RELATIONSHIPS
& SEX EDUCATION
FOR SECONDARY SCHOOLS (2020)

A PRACTICAL TOOLKIT FOR TEACHERS

CRITICAL
PUBLISHING

RELATIONSHIPS & SEX EDUCATION
FOR SECONDARY SCHOOLS (2020)

A PRACTICAL TOOLKIT FOR TEACHERS

Samuel Stones and Jonathan Glazzard

First published in 2020 by Critical Publishing Ltd

British Library Cataloguing in Publication Data
A CIP record for this book is available from the British Library

ISBN: 978-1-913063-65-8

This book is also available in the following e-book formats:

MOBI ISBN: 978-1-913063-66-5
EPUB ISBN: 978-1-913063-67-2
Adobe e-book ISBN: 978-1-913063-68-9

Cover and text design by Out of House Limited
Project Management by Newgen Publishing UK
Printed and bound in the UK by 4edge, Essex

Critical Publishing
3 Connaught Road
St Albans
AL3 5RX

www.criticalpublishing.com

Paper from responsible sources

✚ CONTENTS

➕ MEET THE AUTHORS

JONATHAN GLAZZARD

Jonathan Glazzard is Professor of Inclusive Education at Leeds Beckett University. He is series editor for the Positive Mental Health series by Critical Publishing. Jonathan's research explores issues of inclusion, exclusion, marginalisation, disability, sexuality and mental health for children and young people. He is a researcher, teacher educator and author. Jonathan's background is in primary teaching and he is a trustee of several multi-academy trusts.

SAMUEL STONES

Samuel Stones is a lecturer, researcher and doctoral scholarship student at Leeds Beckett University. He has co-authored texts for several publishers and has written extensively on inclusion and mental health. Samuel's research explores issues of inclusion, exclusion, marginalisation, sexuality and mental health for children and young people. He is a senior examiner and experienced assessor and also holds a national training role with a large multi-academy trust

✚ INTRODUCTION

This book addresses the statutory guidance published by the Department for Education (DfE) for Relationships and Sex Education (RSE) in secondary schools. This guidance replaces previous guidance that was published 20 years ago. The new guidance reflects contemporary societal issues and ensures that young people understand what constitutes healthy relationships, including friendships, intimate relationships and marriage.

The statutory guidance includes important aspects of subject content including consent, sexual harassment, sexual violence, and sexual exploitation and coercion in relationships. In addition, young people must learn about the effects of pornography and online risks including grooming. There is an emphasis on young people understanding the characteristics of unhealthy relationships and on protecting their mental well-being. Abuse, female genital mutilation and honour violence are also identified as subject matter within the statutory guidance. It is important that children learn what is lawful and unlawful.

The guidance states that young people should explore sexual orientation and gender identity 'at a timely point' (DfE, 2019a, p 26) and also that 'schools may choose to explore faith, or other perspectives, on some of these issues in other subjects such as Religious Education' (DfE, 2019a, p 26). A well-designed curriculum will ensure that young people recognise and understand the harmful effects of prejudice-based bullying and stereotypes. There is an emphasis on teaching young people about different types of relationships, including same-sex relationships and same-sex marriage, and on teaching children about the importance of mutual respect and self respect.

Character education is embedded through the guidance so that young people learn about the importance of positive character virtues within the context of relationships. Schools will need to take into consideration that the character virtues that are being promoted through both the formal and hidden curriculum may be different to the character virtues that are promoted within the context of families and communities.

In designing the RSE curriculum, schools will need to ensure that appropriate consultation has taken place with parents. Parents need to know what will be taught, when it will be taught and how it will be taught. Parents retain the right to withdraw their children from Sex Education but not from Relationships Education.

This book addresses the content of the new statutory guidance. There are aspects of the guidance that will be more challenging for schools to address and these are highlighted throughout the book. The content of each chapter is supported by case studies of practice which are designed to support schools to implement the guidance.

✚ CHAPTER 1
FAMILIES

CHAPTER OBJECTIVES

After reading this chapter you will understand:

+ the need to teach students about different types of relationships and families;

+ what to teach students in relation to marriage and the rights and protections it offers;

+ the characteristics of successful parenting and the responsibility of schools to support children to understand these;

+ that students must be taught to recognise and evaluate relationships and be able to report concerns they may have in relation to these.

INTRODUCTION

This chapter outlines the importance of teaching students to recognise and understand different types of families and relationships. It also outlines your roles and responsibilities in relation to supporting students to recognise that their peers may have different experiences in relation to the family structures that they are part of. The chapter offers guidance in relation to each of these to develop your understanding and it provides examples to support your teaching of these topics. The chapter also emphasises the importance of students understanding how relationships can contribute to mental well-being, and the common characteristics of healthy families are outlined. Guidance is provided on the teaching of marriage and some key facts are highlighted to support your planning and delivery of this topic. The requirements of the statutory guidance to teach students to understand the roles and responsibilities of parents are then discussed. Within this discussion the characteristics of successful parenting are outlined to support your teaching. Finally, the chapter argues that students must be taught to evaluate relationships and that they should understand how to seek help and share concerns should they need to.

TYPES OF RELATIONSHIPS

The statutory guidance (DfE, 2019a) states that students should know that there are different types of committed, stable relationships. Students should therefore be taught about heterosexual relationships, same-sex relationships, marriage, civil partnership, co-habiting and other types of relationships. Essentially, regardless of the type of relationship, it is important that students understand how relationships can contribute to mental well-being. Students should be taught to understand that there are different types of families, including families with same-sex parents, foster or adoptive parents and those with single parents. Some children may be raised by siblings or other members of the extended family. Students need to understand that regardless of family structure, there are things that healthy families share in common. These include valuing time together, caring for one another, supporting each other emotionally and/or financially, respect for each family member and demonstrating love and commitment.

CRITICAL QUESTIONS

+ How have views on relationships changed over recent decades?

+ To what extent are commitment and stability important in relationships?

+ Why do you think the government wants students to learn about the importance of committed, stable relationships?

MARRIAGE

Students need to understand that marriage constitutes a legally binding agreement and therefore carries legal rights and protections that are not available to couples who have chosen not to marry or to those who have married in an unregistered religious ceremony (DfE, 2019a). In addition, students need to understand that marriage is an important relationship choice and that it must be freely entered into (DfE, 2019a).

Important facts that students need to know about marriage are stated below.

+ Within marriage each person has a legal duty to financially support the other person.

+ Upon death, the surviving partner automatically inherits their partner's assets.

+ Both people have a legal right to live in the matrimonial home, regardless of who bought it.

+ Marriage must be conferred through a civil or religious ceremony. If it is conferred through a religious ceremony, the service will be conducted by a minister of the religion. If it is conferred through a civil ceremony, the service will be conducted by a registrar.

+ The legal age for marriage is 16 in England and Wales, although parental consent is required for those aged 16 or 17.

+ The 2013 Marriage (Same-Sex Couples) Act legalised same-sex marriage in England and Wales. Prior to this legislation, from 2005 same-sex couples were allowed to enter into a civil partnership, which carried similar rights and protections to marriage.

+ Same-sex couples can marry in a civil ceremony, although they may marry in a religious ceremony if they secure agreement to marry from a religious organisation.

+ Some relatives are not legally allowed to marry.

+ Engagements show intent to marry but have limited status and there is no legal obligation to marry.

+ Marriage can take place in various places including a registered religious building, a registry office, approved premises, at home, a hospital or prison.

+ Bigamy is a criminal offence in England and Wales.

+ Polygamous marriages may not be performed in the United Kingdom.

+ Remarriage is allowed in a civil ceremony providing that the previous marriage has been dissolved.

CRITICAL QUESTIONS

+ How important is marriage within contemporary British society?

+ How do perspectives on marriage vary across cultures and societies?

+ To what extent does the RSE guidance promote marriage as an ideal?

+ Why do you think the government wants students to learn about the importance of marriage?

SUCCESSFUL PARENTING

The statutory guidance (DfE, 2019a) states that students need to understand the roles and responsibilities of parents with respect to raising children and the characteristics of successful parenting. These may include:

+ providing food, clothing and adequate shelter for their children;

+ nurturing the development of positive character virtues;

+ safeguarding their children from emotional/psychological, physical or sexual abuse and neglect;

+ ensuring access to education.

CRITICAL QUESTIONS

+ Are there any other characteristics of successful parenting that you think are important but are not identified on the above list?

+ How do perceptions of successful parenting vary across cultures and societies?

+ To what extent does parenting shape the development of young people's characters?

+ Why do you think the government wants students to learn about the characteristics of successful parenting?

EVALUATING RELATIONSHIPS

It is important that young people can determine whether a relationship within the family is safe or unsafe and to be able to recognise this in other people's relationships. It is also important that students know how to seek help if they feel that a relationship is unsafe and that they know how to report any concerns they have about other people's relationships.

CRITICAL QUESTIONS

+ What are the characteristics of a safe relationship?

+ What are the characteristics of an unsafe relationship?

+ Is it right to intervene in someone's relationship if you have concerns about it?

CASE STUDY

FAMILIES AND OTHER RELATIONSHIPS

YEAR 8, PSHE

The following sequence of lessons is designed to support a Year 8 unit of work which focuses on families.

Lesson 1

In this lesson the students will learn about the importance of stable relationships and they will understand how a stable relationship contributes to well-being.

+ Provide the students with statements on cards about the characteristics of different relationships. Ask them to sort them into 'stable relationships' or 'unstable relationships'.

  Statements

  - You are jealous of your partner.
  - You both love each other.
  - You both trust each other.
  - You jointly make decisions with your partner.
  - You hide things from your partner.
  - You have secrets which you do not tell your partner.
  - You both respect each other.
  - You both treat each other with kindness.
  - You both believe in sexual fidelity.
  - You and your partner have shared interests.
  - You and your partner have different interests.
  - You don't trust each other.
  - You don't like your partner doing things without you.
  - You don't like spending time with your partner.

+ Collect feedback from the students and summarise on a concept map the characteristics of committed and stable relationships.

+ Discuss sexual fidelity. How important is it to a stable relationship? Explain that some people are in stable relationships but also have sexual relationships with other people. These are called 'open relationships' and providing that both partners are in agreement with this then they can still enjoy a stable relationship with each other.

+ Discuss the importance of shared interests in relationships. However, emphasise that partners can have different interests and still enjoy a stable relationship.

+ Give the students some case studies of different types of relationships. Ask them to work in pairs to decide if the relationship is stable or unstable.

+ Discuss each of the case studies with the class and invite the students to give their opinions.

Lesson 2

In this lesson the students will learn about different types of healthy relationships.

+ Introduce the students to a variety of relationship types, including same-sex relationships, marriage, co-habiting, relationships within the family, foster parents, adoptive parents, single parents, friends and acquaintances.

+ Provide the students with a brief description of different types of relationships and ask them to identify what type of relationship is being described.

+ Explain that regardless of the type of relationship, healthy relationships share common characteristics. Ask the students to identify these.

+ Give the students descriptions on cards of healthy and unhealthy relationships using short scenarios (not just intimate relationships). Ask them to sort them into 'healthy' and 'unhealthy' relationships. Ensure that the scenarios cover the full spectrum of relationships.

+ Go through the activity as a class and provide students with feedback.

Lesson 3

In this lesson the students will learn about marriage and the legal rights and protections that are associated with it. Students will learn about acceptable and unacceptable behaviour within marriage.

+ Prepare a presentation that includes the key facts about marriage, including cultural perspectives on marriage (for example, arranged marriages). Explain how marriages are celebrated differently in accordance with people's beliefs and give examples.

+ Explain that healthy marriages are characterised by love, trust, respect, openness, kindness, empathy and support. Alternatively, ask the students to identify the characteristics of a healthy marriage. Are there any other characteristics?

+ Ask the students to identify the characteristics of an unhealthy marriage.

+ Give the students a card-sorting activity and ask them to sort descriptions of marriages into either 'healthy' or 'unhealthy' marriages.

+ Go through the activity as a class.

+ Explain that sometimes people are exposed to risks within marriage. Give an example of what might constitute risky behaviour within a marriage.

+ Place three cards on the wall in separate corners of the classroom with the labels 'risky', 'not risky' and 'some risk'. Read out a description of a marriage and ask the students to stand next to the appropriate card by moving to a corner of the room. Repeat with different scenarios. Provide students with an opportunity to say why they have chosen to stand next to a specific card and invite students to share different opinions.

Lesson 4

In this lesson the students will learn about the characteristics of successful parenting.

+ Provide the students with nine statements to illustrate the characteristics of successful parenting. These are listed below:

  - providing food;
  - providing clothing;
  - providing a home;
  - instilling positive character traits;
  - providing love;
  - protecting children from harm;
  - helping their child to become independent;
  - helping their child to feel confident;
  - ensuring access to education.

+ Ask the students to arrange the statements into a diamond nine arrangement to show levels of importance.

+ Go through the activity with the class, providing the students with an opportunity to move statements from one place to another in the diamond nine arrangement.

Lesson 5

In this lesson the students will learn how to evaluate relationships within families, friendships and intimate relationships, and the importance of consent.

+ Explain to the students about the characteristics of safe families, safe friendships and safe intimate relationships.

+ Explain the importance of consent within relationships. Explain that in this unit, consent within intimate relationships will not be covered because this is addressed in a separate unit.

+ Provide the students with a definition of consent.

+ Discuss the factors that can affect a person's capacity to provide consent. Examples include consuming alcohol or drugs, being subjected to threats, or having low self esteem or disabilities.

+ Read out the following scenario:

Simon and Ryan were both aged 15. They were friends. Simon wanted Ryan to break into a garage to steal a bicycle. At first Ryan refused. Simon persuaded Ryan to drink some alcohol to give him some courage to carry out the break in. Eventually Ryan agreed to carry out the crime.

+ Ask the students to discuss in pairs whether Ryan had given his consent to break into the garage.

+ Explain to the students that although Ryan agreed to break into the garage, his capacity to give consent was impaired by the alcohol. This is an example of coercion within a relationship.

+ Provide the students with a range of scenarios. Ask them to decide whether consent was given for the specific actions described in each scenario. The focus should be on consent within friendships and families rather than in intimate relationships.

+ Go through each of the scenarios and ask the students to justify their decisions.

Lesson 6

In this lesson the students will learn how to support others who are exposed to unsafe relationships.

+ Remind the students about the characteristics of healthy and unhealthy relationships.

+ In this lesson the students will respond to fictitious letters that people have written to a problem page in a magazine.

+ They will be asked to read a letter and discuss it with a partner. Each partner will have a different letter but both students should be given an opportunity to discuss their letter with their partner.

+ The students will then compose a letter as a reply to the problem. They will provide clear advice to help the person to resolve the problem.

+ At the end of the lesson the teacher will read out some of the responses that the students have generated.

CASE STUDY

A WHOLE-SCHOOL APPROACH TO LGBT INCLUSION

YEAR 7, CROSS-CURRICULAR

A secondary school planned to roll out a whole-school approach to LGBT inclusion. The school was a faith school and the decision to implement the whole-school approach was in response to recent incidents of homophobic, biphobic and transphobic bullying.

The bulk of the curriculum work would take place in Year 7. School leaders initially developed a policy in partnership with parents to address LGBT inclusion. A gender-neutral uniform was immediately introduced and changes were made to the physical infrastructure of the school. All the toilets were converted into gender-neutral toilets with separate cubicles and dividing walls that went from the floor to the ceiling. The Year 7 curriculum was modified to ensure that all subject areas addressed LGBT identities and experiences. The history curriculum was modified to include a unit of work on LGBT history. Homophobic, biphobic and transphobic bullying was addressed through drama, and in art students used a range of media to explore the links between mental health and LGBT identities. In science, students were introduced to the work of famous LGBT scientists. In geography, the unit of work on geographical migration explored the migration of LGBT people from rural areas to cities. In maths, students analysed data on the experiences of LGBT people in a unit of work on statistics and data handling. In English, texts were carefully chosen to address specific LGBT themes. In physical education, the department supported the rainbow laces campaign and also developed a broader range of physical activities that had greater appeal to LGBT students. The school library was enhanced and texts that explored LGBT identities were purchased. Notices were placed on noticeboards to communicate the school's zero tolerance policy in relation to homophobic, biphobic and transphobic bullying. In Relationships and Sex Education, students were introduced to same-sex relationships and same-sex marriage. An LGBT student group was introduced to influence whole-school change.

Before any of this work took place, parents were consulted and invited to attend a briefing event at the school. The leadership team ensured that governors were present at this meeting so that parents knew that the governors were in support of the developments. Several of the parents raised objections on the grounds of religion. These parents were invited into school to meet with school leaders who provided them individually with an opportunity to share their concerns. The leaders listened to their views but explained that the school was meeting its legal obligations to students, citing the Equality Act (2010) and the Relationships and Sex Education statutory guidance (DfE, 2019a). Some of these parents chose to remove their children from the school. Curriculum plans, including unit plans and lesson plans, were made available to any parents who requested to view them.

SUMMARY

This chapter has considered the importance of teaching students to understand that different types of families and relationships exist. Specifically, it has outlined the importance of schools and school staff, recognising that students within the school community will themselves have different experiences in relation to their family structure. It is essential that teachers consider this in their planning and delivery so that there is a sense of inclusion among all students and so that they are supported to recognise the different experiences of their peers. It is important to understand whether students are currently taught to recognise the different types of families and relationships that exist so that any gaps in current provision can be identified and prioritised. The chapter has also provided guidance to support you to teach students about marriage. Again, it is important to recognise that students will have different experiences of marriage in their own families. Some students may not understand that same-sex couples are able to marry, and it is essential that students recognise that their peers may live with same-sex parents.

FURTHER READING OR SOURCES OF FURTHER INFORMATION

Public Health England has published learning resources and teacher guidance to support your teaching in relation to the nature of friendships. The materials also guide teachers through the delivery of learning activities that focus on the challenges that may arise in social relationships and the role of peer support in overcoming these. The resource pack includes lesson plans, written guidance and a presentation as well as links to case study videos. The pack, called *Forming Positive Relationships Lesson Plan Pack*, can be found at https://campaignresources.phe.gov.uk/schools/resources/relationships-lesson-plan-pack (accessed 6 February 2020).

In addition to Public Health England, the PSHE Association has also published a wide selection of teacher resources to support the teaching of issues relating to friendships and relationships. These include:

PSHE Association (2016) *Railway Children Resources: Lesson Plans on the Risks of Children Running Away*. [online] Available at: www.pshe-association. org.uk/curriculum-and-resources/resources/railway-children-resources-lesson-plans-risks (accessed 6 February 2020).

PSHE Association (2018) *NSPCC 'Making Sense of Relationships' Lesson Plans and Guidance*. [online] Available at: www.pshe-association.org.uk/ curriculum-and-resources/resources/nspcc-%E2%80%98making-sense-relationships%E2%80%99-lesson-plans (accessed 6 February 2020).

+CHAPTER 2

CHARACTER

CHAPTER OBJECTIVES

After reading this chapter you will understand:

+ the aims of character education;

+ the importance of adopting a whole-school approach to character education;

+ key considerations in relation to the planning and delivery of character education;

+ the importance of culture, behaviour, resilience and confidence;

+ how co-curriculum and volunteering opportunities can contribute to character education;

+ how to promote equality of opportunity within the delivery of character education.

INTRODUCTION

This chapter introduces the concept of character education and emphasises the importance of values, attitudes, skills and behaviours. It also considers the implications of character education within the context of school responsibilities. Additionally, the chapter provides guidance in relation to the key challenges that schools are likely to experience with their planning and delivery of character education. There is some discussion on the importance of character education and this is situated within the requirements of the statutory guidance. The chapter also considers character education in relation to positive school culture and the role of the leadership team is outlined. Some guidance is provided to support schools to develop learners' resilience and confidence and we emphasise the importance of co-curriculum and volunteering opportunities. Finally, the chapter emphasises the role that schools play in promoting equality of opportunity and some guidance is provided to support teachers and school staff.

WHAT IS CHARACTER EDUCATION?

Character education aims to develop a set of values, attitudes, skills and behaviours that support personal development and contribute to positive long-term outcomes (Walker et al, 2017). Specifically, character education aims to support students to develop moral and civic values. This enables them to understand the difference between right and wrong and to understand their responsibilities as citizens to the local and global communities in which they live.

There is no correct approach to delivering character education in schools. However, it is important that school leadership teams view the development of character as being central to the culture, values and vision of the school (Walker et al, 2017). It is also important to adopt a whole-school approach (Walker et al, 2017). This ensures that specific character virtues are consistently reinforced in all classrooms. It is also important that teachers and leaders exemplify the character virtues that they want students to develop (Walker et al, 2017). This has implications for the way in which adults speak to students.

Some students live their lives surrounded by adults in their families and in the wider community who do not demonstrate positive character virtues. It is important to be aware that the values that the school seeks to promote may be in direct conflict with the values that are consistently demonstrated in homes and communities. In this case, students may have to reframe their character traits when they are operating within the context of the school. Some students will internalise the positive character virtues that the school promotes, and these will shape their identities as they develop. Others will learn to 'switch' the positive character virtues on when they are in school, even though they may adopt a different set of virtues when they are outside the school. The key challenge for schools is therefore how to address the dissonance between the character virtues that are promoted outside of school and those that are promoted within schools. More significantly, however, is how schools support students to internalise the positive character virtues that are essential to long-term success so that they consistently demonstrate them, believe in them and subsequently reject the negative character virtues that they may be exposed to outside of school.

CRITICAL QUESTIONS

+ How might social and cultural contexts influence the development of character?

+ Why do you think that character education has become a policy priority?

THE IMPORTANCE OF CHARACTER

Although character education is not identified as a separate strand within the statutory guidance (DfE, 2019a), it is embedded within specific themes. Within the strand of 'respectful relationships', specific character traits are addressed. These character traits include trust, respect, honesty, kindness, generosity, boundaries, privacy, consent, conflict management and skills in reconciliation and ending relationships. In addition, respect for authority is identified as a key character trait. Character education is therefore part of Relationships Education in secondary schools.

The statutory guidance states:

A growing ability to form strong and positive relationships with others depends on the deliberate cultivation of character traits and positive personal attributes, (sometimes referred to as 'virtues') in the individual.

(DfE, 2019a, p 20)

18

Evidence suggests that character education supports the development of a positive school culture, leads to a more conducive learning environment and leads to improved behaviour and attendance and motivation (OECD, 2015; Walker et al, 2017). It also leads to positive long-term outcomes including facilitating access to higher education (Walker et al, 2017) and promotes good mental well-being (DfE, 2019b; Taylor et al, 2017). Character education therefore drives equality and social mobility. Research has found that specific character traits are associated with positive outcomes. These are summarised below.

+ *High self-efficacy is associated with better performance and greater persistence and motivation. Self-efficacy is a prerequisite to investing sustained effort in a task.*

+ *High levels of intrinsic motivation are associated with greater persistence and achievement.*

+ *Good self-regulation, including the ability to delay gratification, is associated with greater attainment.*

+ *High levels of resilience are associated with greater wellbeing.*

+ *Mindsets are malleable and supporting students to develop a growth mindset may result in small to medium size improvements in later performance.*

(Gutman and Schoon, 2013)

Character is a complex concept and multifaceted. Important aspects include:

+ *the ability to stay motivated by long-term goals, including the ability to invest effort and persevere with something despite setbacks;*

+ *the development of moral attributes or virtues;*

+ *the acquisition of social confidence, including the ability to make persuasive arguments, listen to others and demonstrate good manners and courtesy toward others;*

+ *the ability to appreciate the importance of long-term commitments, for example by demonstrating commitment to a relationship, a vocation, a faith or world view or a commitment to the local community.*

(DfE, 2019b)

The *Education Inspection Framework* (Ofsted, 2019) embeds character education within the strand of 'personal development'. Inspectors will evaluate the curriculum and the school's work in supporting learners to develop their character, including their resilience, confidence and independence.

CRITICAL QUESTIONS

+ What character virtues are important to you?

+ What factors shaped the development of your own character?

Research demonstrates that students who are focused on intrinsic-related goals for engaging in an activity show greater motivation, more persistence and higher achievement compared to students who are focused on extrinsic-related goals (Gutman and Schoon, 2013). Studies have shown that the ability to self regulate is a significant predictor of attainment (Moffitt et al, 2011). There is also evidence that teaching students to develop appropriate social behaviour improves attainment (Durlak et al, 2011).

DEVELOPING A POSITIVE SCHOOL CULTURE

School leaders are responsible for creating the school ethos and culture. The school ethos should embody a strong vision for character and personal development (DfE, 2019b). The importance of positive virtues and character traits should be embodied within the school vision. Desirable character traits that might be included in the vision are:

+ *belief in achieving goals;*

+ *persevering with tasks;*

+ *honesty and integrity;*

+ *courage;*

+ *humility;*

+ *kindness and generosity;*

+ *trustworthiness;*

+ *a sense of justice;*

+ *self-respect and self-worth.*

(DfE, 2019a)

Encouraging students to undertake social action, active citizenship and voluntary service to others are excellent approaches for developing these character traits.

DEVELOPING POSITIVE BEHAVIOUR

Research suggests that childhood self control predicts achievement and adjustment outcomes, even in adulthood (Gutman and Schoon, 2013). Good behaviour is an essential characteristic of effective schools. It creates the conditions for effective learning and it prepares students for life after leaving school. Good discipline also ensures that schools are safe places for all members of the school community. An essential aspect of character education is to promote positive social behaviours so that students can learn effectively and are well prepared for adult life.

Students should be taught about the importance of demonstrating respect towards others, regardless of their differences. Demonstrating respect is a fundamental characteristic of an inclusive society. Teaching students about good manners and courtesy ensures that they can conduct themselves appropriately within educational, social and workplace contexts. This is particularly important in cases where students do not live in families or communities where these virtues are demonstrated.

DEVELOPING RESILIENCE AND CONFIDENCE

Students who demonstrate resilience can recover from adverse situations and this can support them in achieving goals. However, the concept of resilience is problematic because resilience is relational. Essentially, this means that a person's ability to be resilient is influenced by their relationships with others. Students are more likely to demonstrate greater resilience if they have access to social support networks that can offer emotional and practical support during challenging times.

Access to supportive teachers, peers, family and community support can enable individuals to be resilient during times when they experience adversity. In addition, resilience is also contextual. Resilience varies from one context to another. It is therefore possible to demonstrate greater resilience in some contexts than it is in others.

The same also applies to confidence. An individual's confidence can vary across social, academic and other domains and it can vary between different contexts. It is also influenced by one's self worth and self efficacy. Self efficacy is an individual's appraisal of their own competences within specific domains, whereas self worth is an individual's overall view of themselves based on evaluations that others (peers, family, teachers) have made on them. Both self efficacy and self worth contribute to overall self esteem. Self esteem is therefore a two-dimensional construct. It is possible for both aspects to be high or low or for one to be high and the other to be low. Overall, self esteem affects confidence.

Resilience and confidence are dynamic traits and are therefore malleable. Supportive school environments can buffer against the effects of negative environments within homes and communities which detrimentally impact on both resilience and confidence. Students can be taught to develop their resilience, for example, by teaching them to recover from 'failure' or teaching them to be resilient to feedback. Exposure to teachers who empower students can dramatically improve a student's confidence. In addition, the experience of academic success is a vital ingredient for improving confidence and self esteem. As students begin to realise that they are capable of achieving, their self efficacy starts to improve. Students can be taught to demonstrate social confidence in specific situations, even if inwardly they do not feel confident. They can be taught how to appear confident but more importantly a skilled teacher can provide students with genuine confidence by getting them to believe in themselves.

Access to a well-designed curriculum helps students to develop confidence. Knowledge and skills should be sequenced correctly. This enables students to make sense of new subject content because correct sequencing provides them with the foundational knowledge and skills upon which new content can be accommodated. In addition, access to a broad and rich curriculum which provides students with cultural capital is essential for developing social confidence and social mobility. One way of achieving this is to develop their vocabulary and knowledge so that students from all social backgrounds can experience and benefit from the same opportunities.

CASE STUDY

STUDENT LEADERSHIP PROGRAMME

YEARS 9 AND 10, PSHE

A secondary school created a student leadership team to support the school with the planning and organisation of key events. The student leadership team also supported induction and transition events for students joining the school as well as organising charitable activities and fundraising events. The team was made up of students from all year groups in the school. The students in Year 12 and Year 13 held senior roles and worked with school staff to develop a peer mentoring programme. These senior students worked with school staff to train students in Years 9 and 10 to become peer mentors for students in Year 7. The peer mentors provided a range of types of support including academic support and social and emotional support. The peer mentors were recruited to the role following an application and interview process which was led by the senior students with support from school staff. Through this process, students were required to demonstrate that they had the necessary character traits to be a good peer mentor. This process was again led by the senior students, but it was monitored by school staff who maintained final responsibility for the decisions that were made. The peer mentors completed a training programme that included guidance on how to be a good listener and when to refer cases to an adult in the school. The training involved role play exercises to support the peer mentors to respond to and communicate with others and to determine when it was appropriate to ask an adult for advice. The peer mentors were also taught about their role in relation to confidentiality and ensuring that they did not promise secrecy to the students they were working with. Following successful completion of the training course, each peer mentor was allocated a caseload of Year 7 students. Mentors met with their mentees during specific timetabled slots at break times, during lunch time and after school as well as at times during the registration period. The programme was co-ordinated by the PSHE lead teacher who monitored the impact of the programme and discussed improvements and changes three times per year.

DEVELOPING THE CO-CURRICULUM

As part of the character education curriculum, schools should ensure that there is strong provision for co-curricular activities. A well-planned co-curriculum can build social confidence and self esteem and improve motivation, attendance and academic outcomes for students (DfE, 2019b). Research demonstrates that participation in outdoor adventure programmes has positive effects on the psychological, behavioural, physical and academic outcomes of young people (Gutman and Schoon, 2013).

Activities may include access to sporting or other physical activities, performance, the arts, volunteering, debating, cooking and participation in service. This is not an exhaustive list. The critical point is that schools should ensure that all students can participate in the co-curriculum, including those who are the most disadvantaged. Barriers to participation may include the direct costs of activities and to address this, schools should subsidise activities to prevent financial constraints becoming a barrier to equal opportunities. The co-curriculum should be designed to enable young people to compete and perform. These opportunities improve social confidence and self esteem.

DEVELOPING AND PROMOTING THE VALUE OF VOLUNTEERING

Volunteering empowers students by enabling them to make a positive contribution to their local community. It helps students to develop a civic mindset and provides them with an opportunity to engage in meaningful work. Students can participate in a range of volunteering opportunities. These may include fundraising activities for local and national organisations, protecting the environment or providing services to elderly people in the local community. Research findings suggest that volunteering produces moderate effects for academic outcomes and small effects for non-cognitive outcomes including social skills, self perceptions, and motivation (Gutman and Schoon, 2013).

CASE STUDY

VOLUNTARY SERVICE

YEARS 7 AND 8, PSHE

A group of Year 12 and Year 13 students in a school created a student leadership team with the support of school staff. The student leadership team decided that they wanted to support students to access volunteering opportunities in the local community. The student leadership team created a working group to support the initiative and they invited local charity representatives into the school to discuss whether they could support the provision. A list of volunteering opportunities was drawn up and from this Year 7 and Year 8 students were able to pick the volunteering opportunities that interested them. The school's careers adviser supported this process of selection to ensure that students were choosing volunteering placements that aligned with either students' interests or aspirations. The careers adviser held overall responsibility for monitoring the programme and overseeing communication between the working group and the local charities. The list of volunteering opportunities has continued to expand, and the school now works with more charitable partners than it ever has before. The school has also committed to the programme by identifying and dedicating time within the existing curriculum to enable students to engage with voluntary opportunities. The school also supports students wishing to access these opportunities during the evening, at weekends or during school holidays. It has introduced a process for supporting parents to discuss these opportunities with the charity directly.

DEVELOPING EQUALITY OF OPPORTUNITY

School leadership teams need to identify the barriers to participation in relation to some of the activities outlined in this chapter. Barriers could include the cost and timing of activities, lack of parental support and lack of confidence in students. Leadership teams should consider how these barriers will be addressed so that students from all backgrounds have opportunities to participate, particularly in the co-curriculum. The co-curriculum provides students from the most disadvantaged backgrounds with cultural capital by developing a broader range of interests, knowledge and skills. Access to a co-curriculum and volunteering improves social confidence and self esteem, which contribute to social mobility.

SUMMARY

This chapter has introduced the concept of character education and it has outlined the responsibility of schools in relation to the promotion of values, attitudes, skills and behaviours. It has also considered the implications of character education within the context of school responsibilities and statutory guidance. Guidance has been provided to support schools with the challenges that they may face with the planning and delivery of character education. There has also been some discussion on the importance of character education and we have considered character education in relation to positive school culture and the role of the leadership team. Some case study material has been offered to support your reflection of existing practice and we have encouraged you to consider the benefits of co-curriculum and volunteering. The chapter has also outlined how teachers and school staff can promote equality of opportunity.

FURTHER READING OR SOURCES OF FURTHER INFORMATION

Department for Education (DfE) (2019) *Character Education Framework Guidance*. London: DfE.

National Foundation for Educational Research (NFER) (2017) *Case Study Report Leading Character Education in Schools*. [online] Available at: www.nfer.ac.uk/media/2067/pace02.pdf (accessed 6 February 2020).

The Jubilee Centre (2017) *A Framework for Character Education in Schools*. [online] Available at: https://uobschool.org.uk/wp-content/uploads/2017/08/Framework-for-Character-Education-2017-Jubilee-Centre.pdf (accessed 6 February 2020).

In addition to the reports and guidance published by these organisations, it is also helpful to consider the discussion offered by www.teachersresourceforce. com. This website outlines the benefits of teaching students about character education. It also offers some practical guidance to support you to teach character education in your classroom and it provides links to additional resources that you may find valuable. The specific blog is available at: www.teachersresourceforce.com/charactereducation.html (accessed 6 February 2020).

+CHAPTER 3

RELATIONSHIPS

CHAPTER OBJECTIVES

After reading this chapter you will understand:

+ the characteristics of healthy relationships;

+ how to teach students about consent;

+ a range of common stereotypes that students should be taught to recognise;

+ the importance of teaching students about bullying and unacceptable behaviour within relationships;

+ the need to support students to understand the purpose of the Equality Act (2010) and the range of protected characteristics.

INTRODUCTION

This chapter outlines some of the characteristics of healthy relationships and it highlights the common challenges that students often experience in relation to friendships. It emphasises the role of parental and peer influence within the context of adolescence and some guidance is offered to support you to teach students about consent. Some case study material is provided to illuminate effective practice in relation to the teaching of consent and critical questions are asked to encourage your reflection. The chapter also provides some discussion in relation to stereotyping to support you to teach students about this concept. Some common types of stereotyping have been stated. The roles and responsibilities of schools are explained in relation to teaching students to understand different types of bullying and some examples are offered to support your understanding of what constitutes bullying and how it can take place. The implications of equality legislation are also outlined, and the chapter emphasises your role in relation to teaching students to recognise these and understand the purpose of equality legislation.

HEALTHY RELATIONSHIPS

Healthy relationships, including friendships, are characterised by trust, respect, honesty, kindness, generosity, boundaries, privacy, consent, conflict management and reconciliation. Adolescence can be a difficult time. It is a stage within the life cycle when many young people are exploring their identities and developing their interests, aspirations, values and beliefs. It is common during this stage for friendships to be dissolved and for new friendships to be established. It is also a time when young people seek greater independence from their parents. Consequently, peer influence can be greater than parental influence during this stage of development. Adolescence can be a time when young people start to take risks and, for many, it is a time for developing personal and intimate relationships and therefore a time for sexual experimentation. Taking all of these things into account, adolescence can be a time when friendships and family relationships are tested to their limits.

CONSENT

Consent is often understood within the context of sexual relationships. However, consent should underpin all healthy relationships, including friendships. A clear definition of consent is provided below:

Consent is agreement which is given willingly and freely without exploitation, threat or fear, and by a person who has the capacity to give their agreement.

(PSHE Association, 2015, p 6)

A person consents to something if they agree by choice, and if they possess the freedom and capacity to make that choice. The concept of sexual consent is addressed in Chapter 7. Consent is underpinned by some key principles. These are outlined below.

+ *It is the person seeking consent who is responsible (ethically and legally) for ensuring that consent is given by another person, and for ensuring that that person has the freedom and capacity to give their consent.*

+ *If consent is not clear, informed, willing and active, it must be assumed that consent has not been given. If consent is not clearly given, or is given and then subsequently retracted, this decision must always be respected. Since people can change their minds, or consent to one thing but not to something else, the seeker of consent must keep assessing whether consent is clear, informed, willing and active. Consent must be seen as an ongoing process, not a 'one-off'.*

+ *In healthy relationships, both parties respectfully seek each other's consent and know that their decision to give or not give consent will be respected. A person is never to blame if their decision not to give consent or to withdraw consent is not respected.*

(PSHE Association, 2015, p 3)

Within the context of healthy friendships, consent must be sought by one person and freely given by another person who has the capacity to provide consent and has been given full information about what they are being asked to do. Capacity to provide consent may be affected by a range of factors including sexual orientation, gender, socio-economic and cultural background and Special Educational Needs and Disabilities. Consent is ongoing and can be withdrawn at any point. If consent is withdrawn then the person who sought the consent must respect this decision.

CASE STUDY

CONSENT

YEAR 7, PSHE

Lesson 1

Provide the students with the following scenarios and asked them to decide if consent was given and to provide justification for their responses.

+ Oliver and Alex were both 14 and had been friends since starting secondary school. Alex tended to adopt the role of leader within the friendship. He liked to make decisions and Oliver was normally happy to comply. Oliver is gay but was not out to anyone. One day Alex and Oliver were in town. Alex spotted a pair of trainers that he wanted but he could not afford to buy them. He proposed that they would both walk into the shop and that Oliver would steal the trainers while he distracted the shop assistant. Oliver agreed but as soon as they walked into the shop he told Alex that he had changed his mind. Alex told Oliver that if he didn't steal the trainers he would disclose Oliver's sexuality to everyone, including Oliver's family. Oliver decided to agree to the theft.

+ Luke and James were 15 years old. They had been friends since starting primary school. Luke's family did not have much money, unlike James who came from a more affluent family. James had started to experiment with drugs and he knew a local drug dealer. He told Luke that if he collected the drugs from the dealer, he would give him some money. Luke was reluctant but eventually James persuaded him to collect the drugs. Luke met the drug dealer once a week and collected the drugs for James. James gave Luke £5 per week for doing this.

+ Ameena and Holly were aged 13 and they were best friends. Holly wanted Ameena to send some offensive comments online to another person who Holly did not like. At first, Ameena refused but Holly told her that if she did not do it she would fall out with Ameena and spread malicious rumours about her. Ameena did not want Holly to do this and therefore agreed to do what Holly wanted.

+ Cameron and Harry were best friends. They were aged 14. Cameron wanted Harry to join a local youth club. Harry asked a few questions about the club to find out more about it and then agreed to join. They visited the youth club once a week.

+ Alice and Ebony were friends. They were aged 13. Alice asked Ebony to go swimming with her every week on a Saturday morning. At first Ebony was not sure if she could commit to this weekly. She discussed it with her parents and then decided that she could commit. She agreed to go swimming with Alice every week.

+ Ryan and Josh were aged 16. Both were friends and identified as gay. Ryan told Josh that he wanted him to kiss him. Josh didn't want to kiss Ryan because he didn't see Ryan in that way and he didn't want to ruin their friendship. Over a period of several weeks Ryan persisted by continually asking Josh to kiss him. One evening Ryan produced some alcohol and they both listened to music and got drunk. Ryan asked Josh to kiss him again. Josh agreed.

Lesson 2

+ Remind the students what consent means. Explain that consent should underpin all healthy relationships and not just intimate/ sexual relationships. Consent is agreement that is given willingly and freely without exploitation, threat or fear, and by a person who has the capacity to give their agreement (PSHE Association, 2015).

+ Introduce the students to the following terms:

  – Coercion: wearing another person down using physical, psychological/emotional threats.
  – Manipulation: engineering a situation to increase someone's vulnerability, for example by getting them drunk.
  – Exploitation: preying on vulnerability by providing money, food, alcohol or drugs.

+ Revisit the scenarios from Lesson 1 and ask the students to decide if consent was influenced by coercion, manipulation or exploitation.

+ Provide students with scenarios on cards and ask them to work as a group to sort them into four sorting hoops: coercion, manipulation, exploitation and consent.

+ Go through the scenarios with the students and ask them to identify if any of the scenarios fit into more than one category.

CRITICAL QUESTIONS

+ How might consent be withdrawn?

+ How might consent be coerced, manipulated or exploited?

STEREOTYPES

Stereotypes based on sex, gender, race, religion, sexual orientation or disability can result in prejudice and can normalise non-consensual behaviour (DfE, 2019a). Stereotypes are socially constructed and are used to describe behaviour that is assumed to be typical. Common gender stereotypes are listed below:

+ boys are more aggressive than girls;

+ girls like to shop and boys like to play football;

+ boys are better at science and girls are better at English;

+ boys don't cry;

+ women are better at looking after children than men are.

CRITICAL QUESTIONS

+ What are the stereotypes associated with sexual orientation?

+ What stereotypes are associated with disability?

+ What stereotypes are associated with race?

+ What stereotypes are associated with religion?

33

CASE STUDY

STEREOTYPES

YEAR 8, PSHE

Lesson 1

Introduce the students to the following terms. Print the terms and definitions on separate cards.

+ *Tomboy: An energetic female whose interests, often in sports e.g. football, clothes, look, activities (e.g. climbing trees), are considered more typical of boys.*

+ *Girly girl: A female who dresses and behaves in a traditionally 'female' way.*

+ *Ladylike: A female who is considered to follow traditional feminine stereotypes, often very polite, elegant and graceful.*

+ *Sissy: A slang term used to describe a male who demonstrates female characteristics.*

+ *Macho: A male who is considered to be strong, sometimes aggressive and traditionally in a powerful role.*

+ *Pansy: An insult used towards gay men, to suggest they are weak, cowardly or feminine.*

+ *Butch: An insult used towards gay women, to suggest they display male characteristics.*

+ *Camp: An insult used towards gay men, to suggest they display female characteristics.*

+ *Metrosexual: A word used to describe a heterosexual (straight) man who pays attention to his appearance, often dressing well or choosing to wear make-up.*

(NSPCC and PSHE Association, 2018)

34

Tasks

+ Ask them to match the terms to the definitions.

+ Discuss the origin of these stereotypes. Where do they come from and why might they be dangerous?

+ Provide the students with a range of scenarios on cards. Each scenario will represent a stereotype. Ask them to group the scenarios into sex, gender, race, religion, sexual orientation or disability stereotypes.

+ Go through the scenarios with the class and ask them to identify if any of the scenarios represent more than a single stereotype.

Lesson 2

+ In this lesson the students will learn how the media perpetuate stereotypes.

+ Provide the students with a range of magazines and ask them to annotate words, phrases and images that reflect gender stereotypes.

+ At the end of the lesson display some of these stereotypes on the visualiser.

Lesson 3

+ Ask the students to imagine that they overhear a conversation between two teenagers. One says, *He is too camp to hang around with us. It will be embarrassing. He is not macho enough to fit into our gang.*

+ Ask the students to identify what is wrong with this.

+ Ask them to identify where the stereotype might originate from.

+ How would they respond if they overheard this conversation? How would they challenge it?

+ Provide the students with a range of extracts from overheard conversations. The conversations should demonstrate stereotyping based on not just gender but also sex, race, religion, sexual orientation or disability. Ask the students to write down a written comment next to each conversation to demonstrate how they might challenge the stereotype through their response.

BULLYING

The statutory RSE guidance (DfE, 2019a) states that students need to know about different types of bullying that can occur within relationships, including cyberbullying, the responsibilities of bystanders to report the bullying and how to get help (DfE, 2019a). Students need to be taught to recognise bullying within relationships by understanding that physical bullying is only one type of bullying. They need to be able to recognise that bullying may also include:

+ emotional bullying, in which perpetrators seek to undermine a person's self worth and self respect;

+ acts of manipulation;

+ acts of micro-aggression, which could include ignoring someone, moving away from someone or other forms of non-verbal bullying;

+ cyberbullying.

Bullying may be homophobic, racist, religious, sizeist, disablist or sexist. People's differences in physical appearance, personality and belief can be the motivator for bullying and therefore the curriculum should cover each of these different aspects. Cyberbullying is bullying that takes place over the internet, including bullying which takes place on social media. It takes a variety of forms. These include:

+ *posting hurtful comments;*

+ *posting videos which are targeted directly at a person to cause distress;*

+ *posting photographs which are designed to cause distress;*

+ *inciting others to make hurtful comments aimed at a person;*

+ *sending hurtful text messages using a mobile phone;*

+ *sending hurtful private messages to a person.*

(Glazzard and Mitchell, 2018)

Students need to understand the impact that bystanders can have. Bystanders who fail to report the bullying that they have observed, either online or offline, increase the power held by perpetrators of bullying. One way of reducing the power is to immediately report the bullying that they have witnessed. If the bullying is conducted online, bystanders can take screenshots of the evidence and report the incident to social media companies or to schools. Students need to understand the mechanisms for reporting bullying in school and systems should be developed to secure the anonymity of the bystander.

BEHAVIOUR WITHIN RELATIONSHIPS

Students need to understand what constitutes healthy behaviour within relationships, including friendships. It is particularly important that students understand that coercion, manipulation, exploitation and violent forms of behaviour are not acceptable within relationships. Students also need to understand that controlling behaviours are also not acceptable. It is important that students know that healthy relationships are based on trust, respect, kindness, consent, honesty and boundaries.

SEXUAL BULLYING

Sexual bullying is any bullying behaviour, whether physical or non-physical, that is based on a person's sexuality or gender. It is when sexuality or gender is used as a weapon (by a person of any sexuality or gender) towards another person. Sexual bullying can be conducted online or offline and can include:

+ sexualised name-calling;

+ verbal abuse;

+ criticising sexual performance or behaviour;

+ ridiculing physical appearance, spreading rumours about someone's sexuality or sexual experiences they have had or not had;

+ unwanted touching and physical assault.

Sexual bullying is behaviour that is repeated over time and intends to hurt someone by using that person's gender, sexuality or sexual (in)experience to hurt them.

Sexual harassment refers to unwanted behaviours that are of a sexual nature. These may include, but are not limited to:

+ behaviour which seeks to intimidate someone or violate their dignity;

37

+ behaviour which seeks to degrade, humiliate or embarrass;

+ behaviour which seeks to create an uncomfortable, hostile or offensive environment.

It is important to understand that an individual does not need to have previously objected to someone's behaviour for it to be legally considered as unwanted. Furthermore, the law states that unwanted behaviours can constitute sexual harassment even if the effect was not intended.

The term 'sexual violence' refers to any kind of unwanted sexual act or activity. Sexual violence includes rape but there are also many other types of sexual violence. These include sexual assault, sexual harassment, female genital mutilation (FGM) and sexual abuse.

Sexual harassment and sexual violence are both forms of sexual bullying. It is important that students are aware of this. However, it is also important that students are taught the difference between the two, and schools play an important role in developing students' understanding of these types of abuse. There are a range of charitable organisations that seek to support schools to teach students about sexual bullying. It is worth contacting local charities to determine the support that is available. These organisations can often provide you with a range of printed resources or materials and may be able to contribute their advice and expertise through visiting speakers and outreach work.

LEGAL RIGHTS AND RESPONSIBILITIES

Students need to understand the implications of the Equality Act (2010). This legislation protects individuals from unfair treatment and promotes a fair and more equal society. It safeguards individuals with protected characteristics from direct or indirect forms of discrimination, harassment and discrimination. The protected characteristics include age, disability, gender reassignment, race, religion or belief, sex, sexual orientation, marriage and civil partnership, and pregnancy and maternity.

SUMMARY

This chapter has offered guidance to support your teaching in relation to relationships and adolescence. It has encouraged you to consider the common challenges that students face in relation to these and to reflect on how your teaching supports students to address these. The chapter has also explained the concept of sexual bullying and it has outlined the role of schools to teach students about sexual harassment and sexual violence. It has emphasised the value of charities and organisations in supporting the teaching of sensitive topics and we have encouraged you to contact those in your local area. It is also important to consider that there may be students in your school who have directly experienced bullying and abuse and that these students may find the topics particularly difficult to discuss in a classroom environment with peers and other adults. Prior to delivering these topics it is important to seek advice and establish a process for supporting students who become upset during the delivery.

FURTHER READING OR SOURCES OF FURTHER INFORMATION

There are many organisations and charities that regularly publish advice and guidance on their websites in relation to the topics in this chapter. These websites include:

Childline. Available at: www.childline.org.uk (accessed 6 February 2020).

NSPCC. Available at: www.nspcc.org.uk (accessed 6 February 2020).

Stonewall. Available at: www.stonewall.org.uk (accessed 6 February 2020).

Young Minds. Available at: www.youngminds.org.uk/find-help/feelings-and-symptoms/bullying (accessed 6 February 2020).

Anti-Bullying Alliance. Available at: www.anti-bullyingalliance.org.uk (accessed 6 February 2020).

Childnet International. Available at: www.childnet.com/young-people (accessed 6 February 2020).

Barnardo's. Available at: www.barnardosrealloverocks.org.uk/secondary-schools/ (accessed 6 February 2020).

+CHAPTER 4

ONLINE AND SOCIAL MEDIA

CHAPTER OBJECTIVES

After reading this chapter you will understand:

+ young people's rights and responsibilities as digital citizens;

+ research findings in relation to social media and mental health;

+ the concepts of cyberbullying, harassment, denigration, flaming, impersonation, outing and trickery, and cyber-stalking;

+ the risks associated with internet usage;

+ the requirement for schools to teach students about pornography and online activity.

INTRODUCTION

This chapter outlines young people's rights and responsibilities as digital citizens. It provides examples of these to support your understanding and it considers fundamental British values with a specific focus on mutual respect. The chapter also offers guidance on what to teach students and some discussion is used to support your reflection. The risks of online activity are identified and the link between online activity and mental health is explained in relation to anxiety, stress and depression. The chapter then introduces you to a range of concepts relating to online activity and case study material is provided throughout the chapter to illuminate effective practice.

DIGITAL RIGHTS AND RESPONSIBILITIES

Young people need to understand their rights and responsibilities as digital citizens. Online citizens have the right to:

+ respect;

+ be safe;

+ be protected from bullying, harassment or other forms of discrimination.

The concept of digital citizenship is particularly important. Online and offline communities are spaces in which people interact through sharing information, providing mutual support and exchanging resources. They are places where fundamental British values should be upheld, particularly the principle of mutual respect. Online citizens have responsibilities to treat people fairly, respect different beliefs and uphold the principles of democracy. Developing students' understanding of these rights and responsibilities links with citizenship education.

Students need to be taught to recognise that the way that they treat people online should not differ from how they treat people offline, assuming of course that they treat people offline with respect. When online, people can hide under a cloak of anonymity and fake profiles. Some people find it easier to say hurtful things online because they are making the comments on a computer rather than saying them directly to a person's face. However, hurtful comments can be extremely damaging and have long-lasting effects. Students also need to recognise that the comments they make can be shared multiple times and that even when they delete a comment, it is never truly deleted from the internet. What goes online stays online and offensive comments or posts can come back to haunt people in the future. Permanent records of comments can be kept in the form of screenshots, which also have a nasty habit of reappearing.

CRITICAL QUESTIONS

+ Why might people behave differently online and offline?

+ What factors influence young people's online behaviour?

ONLINE RISKS

Evidence suggests that social media use can result in young people developing conditions including anxiety, stress and depression (RSPH, 2017). There are various reasons for this, and this section will explore the contributing factors. Research has found that four of the five most used social media platforms make young people's feelings of anxiety worse (RSPH, 2017). Research suggests that young people who use social media heavily, ie, those who spend more than two hours per day on social networking sites, are more likely to report poor mental health, including psychological distress (Sampasa-Kanyinga and Lewis, 2015). Cyberbullying is a significant problem that affects young people. Evidence suggests that seven in ten young people experience cyberbullying (RSPH, 2017).

Cyberbullying exists in a variety of forms. It can include the posting of hurtful comments online, threats and intimidation towards others in the online space and posting photographs or videos that are intended to cause distress. This is not an exhaustive list. Cyberbullying is fundamentally different to bullying that takes place in person. The victim of the bullying may find it difficult to escape because it exists within the victim's personal and private spaces such as their homes and bedrooms. Additionally, the number of people witnessing the bullying can be extremely large because of the potential for online posts on social media to be shared across hundreds, thousands and millions of people. For the victim this can be significantly humiliating and result in a loss of confidence and self worth. Humiliating messages, photographs and videos can be stored permanently online, resulting in the victim repeatedly experiencing the bullying every time they go online. Victims of cyberbullying can experience depression, anxiety, loss of sleep, self harm and feelings of loneliness (RSPH, 2017).

Social media has also been associated with body image concerns. Research indicates that when young girls and women in their teens and early twenties view Facebook for only a short period of time, body image concerns are higher compared to non-users (Tiggeman and Slater, 2013). Young people view images of 'ideal' bodies and start to make comparisons with their own bodies. This can result in low body esteem, particularly if young people feel that their own bodies do not compare favourably to the 'perfect' bodies they see online. Young people are heavily influenced by celebrities and may desire to look like them. If they feel that this is unattainable it can result in depression, body surveillance and low body confidence. Young people can then start to develop conditions such as eating disorders. The issue of body image is not just a female issue. Young males are also vulnerable and influenced by the muscular, well-toned bodies that they see online. We now live in an age when males are taking increasing interest in their appearance, and viewing images of muscular, toned bodies can result in them putting their bodies through extensive fitness regimes. Males are also vulnerable to developing eating disorders. The opportunity for people to use digital editing software to edit their appearance on photographs can also result in young people developing a false sense of beauty. It is worrying that there is a rise in the number of young people seeking to obtain cosmetic surgery (RSPH, 2017) and the popularity of selfies in recent years has resulted in an increase in images that portray beauty and perfection. These images can have a negative impact on body esteem and body confidence.

Research demonstrates that increased social media use has a significant association with poor sleep quality in young people (Scott et al, 2016). It seems that young people enjoy being constantly connected to the online world. They develop 'fear of missing out' (FOMO), which is associated with lower mood and lower life satisfaction (Pryzbylski et al, 2013). This can result in young people constantly checking their devices for messages, even during the night, resulting in broken sleep. Sleep is particularly important during adolescence and broken sleep can result in exhaustion and lack of opportunity for the brain to become refreshed. Lack of sleep quality can have a range of detrimental effects, but it can also impact on school performance and behaviour.

The link between social media use, self harm and even suicide is particularly worrying (RSPH, 2017). The fact that young people can access distressing content online that promotes self harm and suicide is a significant cause for concern. This content attempts to 'normalise' self harm and suicide and can result in young people replicating the actions that they are exposed to.

CASE STUDY

BODY IMAGE

YEAR 7, PSHE

+ Students were shown a range of photographs of people which had been digitally edited. Students were asked to decide what aspects of each photograph might have been edited.

+ Students were then asked to consider the advantages and disadvantages of digitally editing photographs, including the risk of developing low body confidence.

+ Students were provided with tablets and asked to create a 'selfie'. They were then asked to digitally edit the photograph to make the image look better.

+ Students were then shown a range of comments taken from a social media site that young people had posted to each other about body image. Students were asked to reflect on the impact that these comments might have on those people who view the comments.

CYBERBULLYING

Cyberbullying is bullying that takes place over the internet, including bullying that takes place on social media. It takes a variety of forms. These include:

+ *posting hurtful comments;*

+ *posting videos which are targeted directly at a person to cause distress;*

+ *posting photographs which are designed to cause distress;*

+ *inciting others to make hurtful comments aimed at a person;*

+ *sending hurtful text messages using a mobile phone;*

+ *sending hurtful private messages to a person.*

(Glazzard and Mitchell, 2018)

HARASSMENT

Harassment is the act of sending offensive, rude and insulting messages and being abusive. It includes nasty or humiliating comments on posts, on photos and in chat rooms and making offensive comments on gaming sites. Posting false and malicious things about people on the internet can be classed as harassment.

DENIGRATION

This is when someone may send information about another person that is fake, damaging and untrue. It includes sharing photographs of someone for the purpose of ridiculing and spreading fake rumours and gossip. This can be on any site online or on apps. It includes purposely altering photographs of others to ridicule and cause distress.

FLAMING

Flaming is when someone purposely uses extreme and offensive language and deliberately gets into online arguments and fights. They do this to deliberately cause distress in others.

IMPERSONATION

Impersonation is when someone hacks into someone's email or social networking account and uses the person's online identity to send or post vicious or embarrassing material to or about others. It also includes making up fake profiles of others.

OUTING AND TRICKERY

This is when someone shares personal information about someone else or tricks someone into revealing secrets and subsequently forwards it to others. This may also involve the sharing or distribution of private or personal images and videos.

CYBER-STALKING

Cyber-stalking is the act of repeatedly sending messages that include threats of harm, harassment, intimidating messages, or engaging in other online activities that make a person afraid for their safety. The actions may be illegal depending on what they are doing. Cyber-stalking can take place on the internet or via mobile phones. Examples include:

+ silent calls;

+ insulting and threatening texts;

+ abusive verbal messages;

+ cases of stolen identities.

EXCLUSION

This is when others intentionally leave someone out of a group such as group messages, online apps, gaming sites and other online engagement. This is also a form of social bullying and is very common.

BULLYING BY SPREADING RUMOURS AND GOSSIP

Online abuse, rumours and gossip can go viral very quickly and be shared by many people within several minutes. It is not uncommon for former close friends or partners to share personal secrets about victims.

THREATENING BEHAVIOUR

Threatening behaviour that is directed at a victim to cause alarm and distress is a criminal offence. Taking screenshots of the evidence and reporting it is one way of challenging this.

HAPPY SLAPPING

This is an incident where a person is assaulted while other people take photographs or videos on their mobile phones. The pictures or videos are then circulated by mobile phone or uploaded on the internet.

GROOMING

Grooming is when someone builds an emotional connection with a child to gain their trust for the purposes of abuse and exploitation. It is conducted by strangers (or new 'friends') and may include:

+ pressurising someone to do something they do not wish to do;

+ making someone take their clothes off;

+ pressurising someone to engage in sexual conversations;

+ pressurising someone to take naked photographs of themselves;

+ making someone engage in sexual activity via the internet.

Groomers may spend a long time establishing a 'relationship' with the victim by using the following strategies:

+ *pretending to be someone they are not, for example saying they are the same age online;*

+ *offering advice or understanding;*

+ *buying gifts;*

+ *giving the child attention;*

+ *using their professional position or reputation;*

+ *giving compliments;*

+ *taking them on trips, outings or holidays.*

(www.nspcc.org.uk, accessed 30 January 2020)

47

It is against the law for anyone under the age of 18 to take, send or redistribute indecent pictures of anyone under the age of 18. Groomers can be male or female and they can be of any age.

The Child Exploitation and Online Protection Command (CEOP) investigates cases of sexual abuse and grooming on the internet.

INAPPROPRIATE IMAGES

It is very easy to save any pictures of anyone on any site and upload them to the internet. Uploading pictures of someone to cause distress is a form of cyberbullying. This also includes digitally altering pictures to embarrass someone.

BYSTANDER EFFECT

Witnessing cyberbullying and doing nothing about it is not acceptable. Some people are worried about getting involved but victims of bullying need brave witnesses to make a stand. Perpetrators of bullying thrive when they have an audience. Making a stand against what they are doing is one way of reducing their power. Most sites now operate a reporting facility so that online abuse can be reported and addressed. Bystanders are not innocent. They have a responsibility to report abuse that they witness.

CRITICAL QUESTIONS

+ What can schools do to develop students' digital resilience?
+ How can young people protect themselves from online risks?

THE BENEFITS OF SOCIAL MEDIA

Research suggests that young people are increasingly using social media to gain emotional support to prevent and address mental health issues (Farnan et al, 2013). This is particularly pertinent for young people who represent minority groups, including those who identify as lesbian, gay, bisexual or transgender (LGBT), those with disabilities and those representing black and minority ethnic groups. The use of social media to form online digital communities with others who share similar characteristics can be extremely powerful. Young people from minority groups are able to become 'global citizens', thus reducing isolation. Participating in online networks presents them with an opportunity to meet with others who share their identities, to gain mutual support and advice and to gain solidarity. These networks can reduce feelings of loneliness and support the development of a positive, personal identity. They can also support young people to become more resilient to adverse situations, which can help them to stay mentally healthy. While online communities can be beneficial, they also bring associated risks. For example, members of the LGBT networks can become easy targets for abuse, discrimination, harassment and prejudice. It is therefore critical that young people understand how to keep themselves safe online and develop appropriate digital resilience to enable them to address these challenges.

Social media use can allow young people to express themselves positively, letting young people put forward a positive image of themselves. The problem with this is that people tend to use social media to present the best version of themselves and of their lives. This can result in others making unhealthy comparisons between their own lives and the idealised lives that are depicted on the internet, resulting in low self esteem. Social media platforms enable young people to share creative content and express their interests and passions with others (RSPH, 2017). This can help to strengthen the development of a positive identity among young people and provide them with numerous opportunities to experiment with a range of interests. This is particularly important for young people who live in rural communities who may find it more challenging to develop social connections in the offline world. Students living in boarding schools benefit from using social media because it enables them to maintain contact with family members and friends at home. This is particularly important because students living away from home may experience isolation and homesickness, and social media platforms facilitate these connections. Social media platforms offer young people a useful tool to make, maintain or build social connections with others (RSPH, 2017). Additionally, research suggests that strong adolescent friendships can be enhanced by social media interactions (RSPH, 2017). Thus, young people can use social media to cement the friendships that they have formed in the offline world and to develop new friendships that would not have been possible in the offline word due to geographical restrictions.

CRITICAL QUESTIONS

+ Why is social media important to young people?

+ Should schools ban mobile phones?

PORNOGRAPHY

Students in secondary school need to understand how sexually explicit material produces a distorted picture of sexual behaviours. Pornography tends to position women as subservient to men and the sexual activity that is viewed is performed by actors who are paid to carry out a job. It is therefore exaggerated. Aspects that are common in intimate relationships (for example, respect, sexual arousal and consent) are often not evident in pornography and the size of intimate body parts is often not representative of the broader population. In addition, the length of the sexual activity in pornography is often not a true reflection of sexual activity within consenting, intimate relationships. Students need to understand that one of the risks associated with viewing pornography is that the negative behaviours witnessed online may then be replicated by young people within relationships. These behaviours include lack of respect, not seeking consent and power inequalities. Pornography often depicts violence towards women and underplays the importance of feelings and arousal, both of which are important in intimate relationships.

Students need to know the law in relation to pornography.

+ *It is legal to purchase pornographic magazines and videos at 18, and all regulated pornographic websites try to prevent those under the age of 18 from accessing them.*

+ *There are certain types of pornography that are illegal.*

+ *It is illegal for a person under the age of 18 to send explicit images or films of themselves, or of another young person.*

(NSPCC and PSHE Association, 2018)

Pornography can result in unrealistic attitudes about sex and consent and negative attitudes towards roles and identities in relationships. It can result in more casual attitudes towards sex and sexual relationships and an increase in 'risky' sexual behaviour. It can also result in unrealistic expectations of body image and performance (NSPCC and PSHE Association, 2018).

CASE STUDY

PORNOGRAPHY

YEAR 10, PSHE

+ Students were asked to consider the risks associated with viewing pornography.

+ They were provided with a range of possible risks and asked to order these from least important to most important.

+ Students were given a range of scenarios in relation to pornography. These included legal and illegal activity. The students were asked to sort them into both of these categories.

CRITICAL QUESTIONS

+ What challenges might arise in this lesson?

+ How would you address these as a teacher?

ILLEGAL ONLINE ACTIVITY

Students need to understand the law in relation to sharing online content. Creating or sharing explicit images of a child is illegal, even if the person doing it is a child. A young person under the age of 18 is breaking the law if they:

+ *take an explicit photo or video of themselves or a friend;*

+ *share an explicit image or video of a child, even if it's shared between children of the same age;*

+ *possess, download or store an explicit image or video of a child, even if the child gave their permission for it to be created.*

(NSPCC and PSHE Association, 2018)

Schools play a crucial role in supporting students to understand the laws that relate to online activity. It is essential that students are able to determine what is considered legal and what is not. To support students' understanding, it is valuable to deliver an activity that provides students with a selection of legal and illegal scenarios in relation to online activity. These can be sorted into categories.

The following scenarios have been taken from NSPCC and PSHE Association (2018) guidance and adapted to support you to facilitate discussion with students:

+ Brian (19) takes a half-naked photo of his boyfriend (17) and posts it online without his permission.

+ After Sally (21) breaks up with her boyfriend (22), she uses his password to open his social media profile and changes his details, including editing lots of his pictures.

+ Mustafa (17) takes a picture of his genitals and posts it online to entertain his friends.

+ Marla (23) always uses a webcam when she is talking to people she has met in chatrooms.

+ John (22) accepts all friend requests and currently has 950 friends.

+ Georgia (17) kissed Sally (17) when she was passed out at a party. She has a photo on her phone to prove it and shares it with her friends in a group chat.

+ A couple decide to take naked photos of themselves and send them to each other. Both of them have promised they will never show the photos to anyone else.

+ Shahima (15) shares a tablet with her older brother; they both use it to check social media every evening.

SUMMARY

This chapter has outlined some of the common risks that students may experience as a result of their online activities. It has provided examples of these and guidance has been offered to support you to teach students to address the risks that they face. Throughout the chapter, case study material has been provided to equip you with teaching strategies and critical questions have been asked to support your reflection. The chapter has also signposted you to additional sources of support and further information. We recommend that you consider familiarising yourself with these as there are many organisations that are able to support schools with the planning and delivery of these topics.

FURTHER READING OR SOURCES OF FURTHER INFORMATION

Barnardo's has released guidance to support schools to deliver high-quality, age appropriate Relationships and Sex Education. Their advice can be accessed at: https://b.barnardos.org.uk/fv_sre_campaign_qa_final_10th_jan.pdf (accessed 6 February 2020).

The NSPCC has worked with the PSHE Association to create a sequence of lessons that are suitable for Key Stage 4 students. The resources and supporting materials cover a range of key topics, including:

+ transition to secondary school;
+ online safety and online friendships;
+ consent, sexualised behaviour;
+ unhealthy relationships;
+ sharing sexual images.

The resource packs also offer guidance to teachers on creating a safe learning environment and what to do in the event of receiving a disclosure. The materials highlight additional support and a letter is provided that can be used to inform parents about the content and purpose of lessons. The materials can be accessed for free at: https://learning.nspcc.org.uk/research-resources/schools/making-sense-relationships/ (accessed 6 February 2020).

✚CHAPTER 5

BEING SAFE

CHAPTER OBJECTIVES

After reading this chapter you will understand:

+ the key principles of consent;

+ how to teach students about consent;

+ the concepts of sexual exploitation, grooming, coercion, harassment and rape;

+ the need to teach students to understand domestic abuse, forced marriage, honour-based violence and female genital mutilation;

+ key legislation in relation to online safety.

INTRODUCTION

This chapter outlines the principles of consent and it provides key definitions to support your understanding. It provides guidance in relation to the teaching of consent and case study material is offered to illuminate effective practice. The chapter then explores the concepts of sexual exploitation, grooming, coercion, harassment and rape. It provides some discussion in relation to each to support you to teach students about these. The legal definition of rape is explained and a range of myths in relation to rape are highlighted. Some critical questions are asked to support you to reflect on your current understanding and the implications of these for your teaching. The chapter also discusses your role in relation to teaching students to understand forced marriage, honour-based violence and female genital mutilation. Finally, the chapter outlines some legislation in relation to online safety and the importance of students being taught to recognise the risks associated with online activity.

CONSENT

According to the PSHE Association (2015, p 3) *'learning about consent should begin before young people are sexually active, otherwise it is too late'*. The key principles of consent are outlined below.

+ *It is the person seeking consent who is responsible (ethically and legally) for ensuring that consent is given by another person, and for ensuring that that person has the freedom and capacity to give their consent.*

+ *If consent is not clear, informed, willing and active, it must be assumed that consent has not been given. If consent is not clearly given, or is given and then subsequently retracted, this decision must always be respected. Since people can change their minds, or consent to one thing but not to something else, the seeker of consent must keep assessing whether consent is clear, informed, willing and active. Consent must be seen as an ongoing process, not a 'one-off'.*

+ *In healthy relationships, both parties respectfully seek each other's consent and know that their decision to give or not give consent will be respected. A person is never to blame if their decision not to give consent or to withdraw consent is not respected.*

(PSHE Association, 2015, p 3)

Key definitions are stated below.

+ **Consent** is agreement that is given willingly and freely without exploitation, threat or fear, and by a person who has the capacity to give their agreement.

+ **Sexual consent** refers to a positive choice to take part in a sexual activity by people who understand the nature and implications of the activity they are agreeing to.

In addition:

+ *consent must be free – an active, personal choice;*

+ *consent must not be inferred, assumed, coerced or gained by exploitation;*

+ *the person giving consent must have the capacity to do so;*

+ *it is the person seeking consent who is legally and ethically responsible for ensuring that consent is given and meets these criteria;*

+ *the seeker of consent should not see seeking consent as a 'one-off' but rather a continuing process of making sure the other person is consenting;*

+ *the key signs of consent are that the person clearly wants to engage in the activity and actively demonstrates this verbally and/or through their body language;*

+ *not saying 'no' is not giving consent;*

+ *consent should be explored in the context of pupils learning about healthy relationships and this should not be solely limited to situations of a sexual nature.*

(PSHE Association, 2015)

When you are teaching students about consent it is important to draw on related concepts. These include mutual respect, empathy, personal safety, and bullying and abuse. It is also important that students are taught about risk. Students must recognise that it is important to be curious and adventurous but at the same time they also need to understand how to keep themselves safe. Schools have a responsibility to teach students to understand how to manage and mitigate risks. It is therefore crucial for teaching to focus on supporting students to take positive and well-considered risks at an appropriate time and with a focus on maintaining personal safety. When you are teaching about risk and consent, you should reinforce that although people take risks, they are never to blame when others fail to respect their decision to withhold or withdraw consent (PSHE Association, 2015). Furthermore, when teaching students about consent and the concepts it links to, it is important to support students to understand common myths, assumptions and misunderstandings. To support your teaching, you may find it valuable to draw on real-life examples to illustrate these. For example, sexual images that may be shared through the internet are often widely available but often depict scenarios where it is not necessarily clear that consent has been negotiated (PSHE Association, 2015).

Teachers have a responsibility to consider the needs of their students and to ensure that lessons and teaching activities are appropriate and build on students' prior knowledge. This enables schools to determine how to teach students about consent and it allows teachers to be responsive to the needs of students. However, it is important to ensure that all lessons are effective and meaningfully planned. This means that all lessons should:

+ *be delivered in a safe learning environment;*

+ *enable students to build on and develop existing knowledge;*

+ *provide opportunities for students to ask questions and raise concerns;*

+ *be taught by teachers with appropriate knowledge and expertise;*

+ *be taught by teachers who have access to and support from colleagues;*

+ *be responsive to students' circumstances and experiences;*

+ *highlight unrealistic norms and the implications of these;*

+ *recognise the influence of social media and the sharing of pornography and images of a sexual nature;*

+ *be supported through the use of realistic scenarios that are not reflective of teachers' or pupils' personal circumstances.*

(PSHE Association, 2015)

CASE STUDY

SEXUAL CONSENT

YEAR 11, PSHE

The students were provided with a range of scenarios to explore sexual and non-sexual consent. They were asked to read the scenarios in pairs and to consider whether consent was given in each of the cases.

+ Someone has previously provided consent, which means that they will always agree to it.

+ Once someone has given consent it cannot be withdrawn.

+ In some cases, there are valid excuses for not respecting someone's right to withdraw consent.

+ Someone didn't give consent, but I thought they were joking because they laughed when they said, '*I don't want to*', so I don't think it matters.

+ Someone was intoxicated and unable to give consent, so I can assume that they would, because they have said yes before.

SEXUAL EXPLOITATION

The legal age of consent is 16. Any sexual activity with a child under the age of 16 is against the law. Child sexual exploitation is when people use their power to sexually abuse children. Sexual abuse covers penetrative sexual acts, sexual touching, masturbation and the misuse of sexual images, such as on the internet or by mobile phone. Sexual exploitation also occurs within relationships when consent is not sought or respected.

When you are teaching students about sexual exploitation it is important to draw on students' prior knowledge of consent. It is also important to consider these topics alongside abuse. It is important to consider these because students need to recognise the relationship between sexual exploitation and consent and between sexual exploitation and abuse. Students must also understand that sexual exploitation may involve young children and it may exist within the digital and online environment. If students are not taught about these risks then they are left unprepared and unprotected should they ever be approached by a perpetrator. Students must know how to report concerns and it is important that they understand how to seek support at all times of the day and regardless of whether they are in the school building with access to school staff.

When you teach students about sexual exploitation you must consider the needs, circumstances and personal experiences of your students. It is important to establish a safe learning space in which students feel able to ask questions and share any concerns with you. You should also ensure that students understand that the classroom is a non-judgemental space.

GROOMING

Grooming is when a person builds a relationship or develops trust and emotional connectivity with a child so they can manipulate, exploit and abuse them. Students must recognise that they can be groomed by people they know and that many perpetrators of sexual abuse have been known to the children that they targeted. Students need to recognise the importance of being careful and alert with everyone and that this includes those that they trust. However, it is also important that students do not become unduly anxious and unable to develop trusting relationships with peers and adults for fear of being abused. This can make it incredibly difficult to teach students about grooming. However, to support your teaching, it is useful to teach students about common signs associated with grooming:

+ groomers pretend to be your friend and may try to build trust with you over a long period of time;

+ groomers may use games and jokes to test your boundaries and see how far they can push you without alarming you;

+ groomers may move from social contact, including hugging, to accidental touching and then to intimate touching over a long period of time;

+ groomers may encourage you to break rules so that they can blackmail you in the future;

+ groomers may encourage the consumption of drugs and alcohol so that it is more difficult for you to object or react;

+ groomers may share sexual material to test your reaction;

59

+ groomers may ask you to communicate secretly or through applications that do not keep logs and copies of your conversation;

+ groomers may blame you for their abuse or try to confuse you by telling you that you like the attention.

These scenarios and examples can be used to teach students to recognise uncomfortable or dangerous situations. Students must also be taught how to respond to these. Within your teaching you should also teach students how to recognise the signs of a situation that may become uncomfortable or dangerous but has not yet fully developed.

COERCION

Coercion is the use of various strategies including intimidation, physical threats or emotional threats to force someone to do something. Coercion can involve threatening to break a confidence. When exploring this concept, students should learn that regardless of what is actually said, agreement sought or given under coercion is not consent. It is also important for students to recognise that a refusal to give consent does not require justification to others. Failing to provide consent is a personal choice that should be respected. Forcing someone to do something when consent has not been provided is coercion. Students need to be supported to recognise coercion within the context of unhealthy relationships, including intimate relationships and friendships.

HARASSMENT

The term 'harassment' is used to refer to unwanted behaviours that occur with the intention or effect of violating an individual's dignity or creating an environment that an individual finds intimidating, hostile, degrading, humiliating or offensive. Students must understand that harassment can occur online and offline and that it does not need to take place face-to-face or within a physical space. It is important to emphasise within your teaching that harassment can be between children, between adults or between an adult and a child.

Students need to be able to identify the common signs of harassment, including:

+ telling stories and spreading rumours;

+ making lewd comments;

+ making remarks about someone's appearance;

+ name-calling;

+ making comments about family members;

+ unwanted messages;

+ coercion and threats;

+ non-consensual sharing of material.

Schools have a responsibility to teach students to recognise and report sexual harassment. Schools must also ensure that they challenge all instances of sexual harassment. Failure to do so can normalise inappropriate behaviours and this may provide an environment that leads to sexual violence (DfE, 2015).

RAPE

According to the law, only a man can commit rape as the penetration has to be with a penis. However, both women and men can be raped. Rape can occur within a relationship or within a marriage. The law says that person A is guilty of rape if:

+ he intentionally penetrates the vagina, anus or mouth of person B with his penis;

+ person B does not consent to the penetration; and

+ person A does not reasonably believe that person B consents.

The legal position in England and Wales is that women can carry out sexual assault (or assault by penetration, which carries the same sentencing) but not rape according to the legal definition. Sexual assault is when any male or female intentionally touches another person sexually without his or her consent.

MYTHS ABOUT RAPE

Students may develop several myths about rape which need to be challenged. These are listed below and taken from PSHE Association guidance.

+ *If someone is raped while drunk, they are at least somewhat responsible.*

+ *If someone dresses provocatively, they are asking for trouble.*

+ *Someone who teases someone else deserves anything that then happens.*

+ *If you go back to someone's house, you are saying you want to have sex with that person.*

+ *When people are raped it is because they haven't said 'no' strongly enough.*

+ *Men don't usually intend to force sex on anyone but sometimes they get carried away.*

+ *If someone engages in kissing or intimacy and then lets things get out of hand, it's their own fault if their partner forces them to have sex.*

+ *Many so-called rape victims are actually people who had sex and 'changed their minds' afterwards.*

+ *People are almost never raped by their partners.*

+ *Rape only happens to women.*

(PSHE Association, 2015)

CRITICAL QUESTIONS

+ What mental image do you hold of a rapist?

+ To what extent is this image based on a stereotype?

+ What sensitive issues might arise when teaching students about rape?

DOMESTIC ABUSE

Domestic abuse is an incident or pattern of incidents of controlling, coercive, threatening, degrading and violent behaviour, including sexual violence, by a partner or previous partner. It includes:

+ coercive control;

+ psychological and/or emotional abuse;

+ physical abuse;

+ sexual abuse;

+ financial abuse;

+ harassment;

+ stalking;

+ online or digital abuse.

When you are teaching students about domestic abuse it is important to consider that some of your students may have had experiences of living in situations that have involved domestic abuse. Some students may also live in households that are currently affected by domestic violence. Throughout your teaching you should signpost support services and you should emphasise that students can discuss their concerns with any member of school staff. Teachers should promote positive relationships in the classroom that are built on trust and safety and this will support students to discuss any concerns that they may have in relation to the topic.

CRITICAL QUESTIONS

+ What might be the signs of the early stages of domestic abuse within a relationship?

+ What impact might domestic abuse have on the victim?

+ What sensitive issues might arise when teaching students about domestic violence?

CASE STUDY

DOMESTIC ABUSE

YEAR 11, PSHE

The students had been taught about healthy relationships and unhealthy relationships and the teacher had introduced the concept of domestic violence by discussing its definition. The teacher provided a range of scenarios that students were asked to discuss and then group into healthy relationships and unhealthy relationships. The students were also asked to identify the scenarios that involved signs of domestic abuse. The scenarios included:

+ a partner encouraging me to keep trying to complete a task which I find hard;

+ a partner making me do things I do not want to do;

+ a partner making me feel bad because I am overweight;

+ a partner listening to me but often disagreeing with my views;

+ a partner stopping me from seeing my friends and family;

+ a partner looking through my phone regularly;

+ a partner asking for my opinion but often ignoring it;

+ a partner making me feel scared when they are drunk;

+ a partner making me feel like I cannot have friends.

FORCED MARRIAGE

A forced marriage is a marriage in which one or both people do not consent to the marriage. The right to refuse is taken away and one or both individuals are coerced into the marriage under duress. Forms of duress include physical, psychological, financial, sexual or emotional pressure to get married. It is a criminal offence in the United Kingdom.

CRITICAL QUESTIONS

+ What sensitive issues might arise when teaching students about forced marriage?

+ How might you address these issues?

HONOUR-BASED VIOLENCE

Honour-based violence is used to control behaviour within families or communities to protect perceived cultural and religious beliefs and/ or honour. Perpetrators of honour-based violence perceive that an individual has shamed the family and/or community by breaking their honour code. Unlike other forms of violence, honour-based violence is often approved of by other members of the family or community. Reasons for breaking the honour code include:

+ wearing inappropriate make-up or dress;

+ entering into an LGBT relationship or identifying as LGBT;

+ rejecting a forced marriage;

+ becoming pregnant outside of marriage;

+ being a victim of rape;

+ demonstrating intimate behaviour or affection in public spaces;

+ participating in alcohol and drug use.

CRITICAL QUESTIONS

+ What sensitive issues might arise when teaching students about honour violence?

+ How might you address these issues?

FEMALE GENITAL MUTILATION (FGM)

FGM is the partial or total removal of the external female healthy genitalia or other injury to the female genitals. There are no reported associated health benefits. Teachers may feel that this is a difficult topic to discuss with students given its shocking nature. However, to challenge and stop this abuse, it is essential that all is done to raise awareness to change attitudes and correct any misconceptions that may be held in relation to FGM. As part of your teaching you should ensure that students are aware that the procedure can be performed at a variety of ages including on those who are adolescent.

It is also important to remember that you may teach students who have themselves been directly or indirectly affected by FGM. As with many of the topics within this chapter, it is important to establish a safe learning environment in which students feel able to share concerns and ask questions.

CRITICAL QUESTIONS

+ What sensitive issues might arise when teaching students about FGM?

+ How might you address these issues?

ONLINE SAFETY

Students should learn that it is illegal to produce, possess or distribute an indecent image of a person under the age of 18. They must also recognise that this law applies to any indecent material of themselves. Teachers should support students to think about and understand the consequences of creating, sharing and sending indecent images and videos. This involves providing advice to students to manage a situation where they are worried about an image or video they have taken of themselves or of others becoming available on the internet.

SUMMARY

This chapter has outlined the concept of consent and it has provided common definitions to support your understanding. Guidance has also been offered to support your teaching of this topic. Additionally, the chapter has explored the concepts of sexual exploitation, grooming, coercion, harassment and rape, as well as forced marriage, honour-based violence and female genital mutilation. Throughout the chapter, case study material has been offered to illuminate effective practice and critical questions have been asked to encourage you to reflect. The chapter has outlined your roles and responsibilities as a teacher, and it has also emphasised the importance of ensuring that all teaching is responsive to the individual needs of all students. We have regularly emphasised that it is important to remember that your students may have personal experiences of the topics that you are teaching and that it is essential to create a safe environment in which students feel able to ask questions and share concerns.

FURTHER READING OR SOURCES OF FURTHER INFORMATION

A range of charitable organisations offer support to schools to teach students about safety. This support may include published guidance and materials and it may involve charities visiting schools to share their expertise.

Victim Support is an example of one charity that regularly publishes material to support your understanding of the topics that have been discussed in this chapter. Their advice and guidance on domestic abuse and recognising its signs is available at: www.victimsupport.org.uk/crime-info/types-crime/domestic-abuse/recognising-signs-domestic-abuse (accessed 6 February 2020).

The UK Safer Internet Centre has also published guidance and teaching materials to support your understanding of the risks associated with online activity. These are available at: www.saferinternet.org.uk/advice-centre/teachers-and-professionals/teaching-resources/sexting-resources (accessed 6 February 2020).

A lesson plan and supporting materials to support your teaching of female genital mutilation have been published by Healthy Schools and can be found at: www.pshe-association.org.uk/system/files/KS3%20FGM%20Lesson%20Plan.pdf (accessed 6 February 2020).

Additional sources of information include:

Department for Education (DfE) (2015) *Sexual Violence and Sexual Harassment between Children in Schools and Colleges*. London: DfE.

PSHE Association (2015) *Teaching about Consent in PSHE Education at Key Stages 3 and 4*. London: PSHE Association.

UK Safer Internet Centre. Available at: www.saferinternet.org.uk (accessed 6 February 2020).

+CHAPTER 6

PHYSICAL HEALTH AND MENTAL WELL-BEING

CHAPTER OBJECTIVES

After reading this chapter you will understand:

+ what is meant by the term 'mental well-being';

+ the common types of mental ill-health;

+ the impact of social media on debt, gambling and body image concerns;

+ the importance of physical activity to support mental health;

+ key considerations in relation to substance abuse, health and prevention, basic first aid and adolescence.

INTRODUCTION

The statutory guidance emphasises the need to teach young people about the steps that they can take to support their own health and well-being. Young people need to understand the importance of self care, physical activity and social connectivity. In addition, they need to understand how participation in hobbies, interests and the community can support them to stay mentally healthy. This chapter provides advice and guidance to support you to meet the requirements of this statutory guidance and it provides case study material throughout to illuminate effective practice. The chapter also offers critical questions to encourage your reflection.

MENTAL WELL-BEING

According to the World Health Organization:

Mental health is a state of well-being in which an individual realizes his or her own abilities, can cope with the normal stresses of life, can work productively and is able to make a contribution to his or her community.

(WHO, 2018)

Students should be taught about ways of improving well-being, including the importance of forming social connections and the role of physical activity, community participation and voluntary service in improving mental health.

Young people also need to be taught to recognise common types of mental ill-health, including anxiety, depression and self harm. A well-designed mental health curriculum supports students to recognise mental ill-health in themselves and others. It facilitates young people's understanding of resilience and provides them with useful strategies to adopt if they experience specific forms of mental ill-health. Additionally, students should learn how to support others by developing empathy and their skills in sensitive, deep listening. Male students need to understand the importance of expressing their feelings and emotions rather than conforming to traditional gender stereotypes.

69

CRITICAL QUESTIONS

+ Which students might be particularly vulnerable to developing mental ill-health?

+ How does the outdoors, including access to nature, support mental health?

CASE STUDY

MENTAL HEALTH

YEAR 8/9, PSHE

In 2018, Cambridge United Community Trust and Leeds Beckett University worked in partnership to evaluate a mental health intervention programme that was delivered in secondary schools to students in Years 8/9. The programme was a six-week intervention which explored a range of themes including developing students' understanding of what mental health is, resilience, anxiety, stress and depression. Students also explored the relationship between social media and mental health. The sessions were delivered by sports coaches from the football club.

Students were interviewed to collect their perspectives on the intervention. These were analysed and grouped into themes. Comments from students are given below.

+ What is mental health?

Mental health is good and bad. Poor mental health for example is when someone is feeling depressed. But depression is not the same as just feeling a little bit sad. When you are depressed it can stop you doing things, like you might not want to get out of bed.

(Student, Year 9)

Depression is not the same as sadness. I have been depressed and it stopped me from going into school. It made me have anger problems. My grades went down. Depression is a form of mental illness.

(Student, Year 9)

+ Ways of improving mental health

There are ways to improve your mental health. You can talk to people who are close to you. If you have a schedule, then it keeps you more organised. Then you don't get stressed.

(Student, Year 9)

It is really important to talk to other people. If you don't let your emotions out it will just get worse. Sometimes it is easier to talk to parents than a teacher or you can talk to people that you trust. You can also talk to your siblings. You don't have a deeply personal connection with your teachers like you have with your friends, so it is easier to talk to friends.

(Student, Year 9)

+ Managing stress

If you are feeling stressed, you can do things to help. You can talk to a teacher, go for a walk, listen to music. Stress can be good and bad at the same time.

(Student, Year 8)

If you use your energy through exercise it can help you to manage your stress. You can do something else like watch TV to take your mind off it. Sometimes you can be stressed when there are too many deadlines, but you can try to get things done rather than letting things stack up.

(Student, Year 9)

+ Knowledge of vulnerable groups

It is harder for men because if they get too emotional, they might feel like they should not be doing that. Men sometimes think they have to be strong. This comes from stereotypes.

(Student, Year 8)

Athletes can get injured and this can make them stressed and they may worry they are letting down their team and supporters. They have a lot of pressure to perform so they can get stressed. LGBTQ people are at risk because some people think they are different.

(Student, Year 9)

71

+ Resilience

Facing a situation that may be difficult but being able to see it through with the best outcome.

(Student, Year 9)

Resilience is when you don't give up and you keep going. You can bounce back from things like failing a test. Resilience helps you to achieve things. It changes your mindset into a positive mindset.

(Student, Year 8)

+ Social media

You can talk to your friends and family on social media. The disadvantages are that you can get stalked. People can create fake accounts. You can get cyberbullied. People can hack into other people's accounts and you might not know who is communicating with you. People can become jealous of other people's lives and this can make you sad and depressed.

(Student, Year 9)

Some of the pictures can be fake so people can make out that they are leading an exciting life, but really they are not, and this can make others feel worthless.

(Student, Year 8)

The research demonstrated that the students valued the intervention. The involvement of the football club was particularly powerful because this provided an opportunity for footballers to talk to students about their own experiences of mental ill-health.

A copy of the full evaluation report can be found at https://leedsbeckett. ac.uk/-/media/files/School-of-Education/mind_your_head_evaluation_ report.pdf (accessed 7 February 2020).

INTERNET SAFETY AND HARM

Students need to be taught about the role of social media in debt, gambling and body image concerns. These reflect current societal issues.

Many young people are heavily influenced by images that depict ideal bodies, and males can be influenced by these images as well as females. The popularity of 'selfies' and celebrities has created opportunities for young people to aspire to look like others. The curriculum should educate students about the use of digital editing software which improves appearances and the importance of respecting everyone regardless of appearance. Students also need to recognise the role of the internet in supporting access to activities which may lead to debt and promote gambling. Students should be aware that these activities are age-restricted and may be addictive as well as illegal or unregulated. Students should understand how to seek support if they are worried about their online activities or if they are worried about the activities of peers.

CRITICAL QUESTIONS

+ Why do you think that body image has become a major concern in recent years?

+ How can young people protect themselves from online risks?

HEALTH AND FITNESS

Both the physical and mental health benefits of engaging in physical activity for adults, as well as for children and young people, are well documented and widely and internationally accepted (Hyndman et al, 2017; McMahon et al, 2017). Physical activity improves fitness and well-being. Students need to understand the benefits of a healthy lifestyle through exercise and good nutrition and they need to understand the link between inactivity, ill-health and disease. It is important that students do not develop obsessions about body image and diet, and that they understand that it is acceptable occasionally to eat foods that have a high fat and sugar content.

CRITICAL QUESTIONS

+ Why might some young people be physically inactive?

+ Why might some students eat unhealthy diets?

+ How can schools support these students to develop healthier lifestyles?

CASE STUDY

PHYSICAL ACTIVITY

YEARS 8–13, PE

Staff in a secondary school PE department identified several students who did not enjoy participating in PE lessons. Some of these students regularly attempted to be excused from the lesson by presenting a note from their parents. Some students with a diagnosis of autism did not enjoy participating in team games. They also disliked the sensation of getting hot and the feel of perspiration on their skin due to their sensory sensitivities. Some students who identified as LGBT did not enjoy participating in games in which gender stereotypical behaviours were displayed during lessons. This made them feel uncomfortable.

The department lead was concerned that these students were not benefitting physically or mentally from physical activity. To address the issue, a wider range of physical activities were introduced, including individual rather than team sports. Students were given the opportunity to participate in boxing, using the treadmill and weightlifting. A climbing wall was also erected. These activities provided an opportunity for students to compete against themselves rather than competing against each other. As the activities were individual sports, this allowed the students to take a break when they needed one to reduce the sensation of feeling hot and sweaty.

In addition, the department introduced a programme of peer mentoring. Older students from Years 12 and 13 were trained as physical activity peer mentors. They led weekly physical activity sessions for younger students who were identified as less physically active. Through this they developed planning, organisation and leadership skills. The younger students enjoyed physical activity more when it was led by a mentor rather than being led by a teacher and their physical activity levels improved. These were small group sessions, which enabled students to build relationships and establish social connections.

SUBSTANCE MISUSE

Young people in secondary schools will be aware of drugs. Drug, alcohol and tobacco use may be prevalent in their homes and communities, and some students may already be experimenting with these. It is important that students understand the relationships between substance use, mental health and disease, including the link between tobacco use and lung cancer. They need to be taught about the physical and psychological consequences of addiction, including alcohol dependency. Students should be taught the facts about legal and illegal drugs and ways of giving up smoking.

Teaching about substance misuse can be challenging, particularly if students already have an addiction or if substance use is evident within their families and communities. Teachers should focus on the facts by highlighting the associated health risks. It is important to create a positive climate which supports students to openly disclose their addictions. If the climate is non-judgemental, young people will be more likely to reach out for support. Providing students with small-group support sessions through which they can learn to break unhealthy habits is an effective way of helping young people. They will often be well-aware of the associated risks, but they may need practical solutions to break the habits that they have formed.

CRITICAL QUESTIONS

+ Why might some young people be experimenting with substance misuse?

+ How can schools support these students to break their habits?

HEALTH AND PREVENTION

Students should understand the importance of good oral hygiene and of regular self examination and screening. It is important that students understand how to check specific body organs to identify possible disease, including the genitals and breasts. Students also need to understand the importance of immunisation, vaccination and good quality sleep. Students need to understand the link between social media use and sleep quality and the effects of sleep deprivation. In addition, they should be taught about the importance of maintaining personal hygiene.

CRITICAL QUESTIONS

+ Why might some students demonstrate poor personal hygiene?

+ How can schools support families to develop healthier lifestyles?

BASIC FIRST AID

Students should be taught how to provide basic treatment for common injuries, life-saving skills and how to administer Cardiopulmonary Resuscitation (CPR). They also need to understand the role of defibrillators and to identify when one might be needed. The school will need to provide a programme of first aid training, delivered by an external organisation.

THE CHANGING ADOLESCENT BODY

Students need to understand the key facts about puberty and the changing adolescent body, including menstrual well-being. They need to know the main changes that take place in the adolescent body and the implications of these for emotional and physical health.

SUMMARY

This chapter has outlined the roles and responsibilities of schools in relation to teaching students about mental well-being. It has provided case study material to illuminate effective classroom practice, and critical questions have been asked to encourage you to reflect on your current understanding of key issues. The chapter has also highlighted common problems associated with internet use and online activities and it has emphasised the need for students to recognise these issues and to be able to seek support if they have concerns. Guidance has been provided to support your understanding of substance abuse and some key considerations have been outlined to support your teaching of this topic. Finally, the chapter has also highlighted the need to teach students about health and prevention, basic first aid and adolescence.

FURTHER READING OR SOURCES OF FURTHER INFORMATION

A wide range of charities offer support to schools in relation to the teaching of the topics in this chapter. One of these organisations is the National Institute on Drug Abuse for Teens, which has published guidance, lesson plans and learning resources to support the teaching of substance abuse. These can be found at: https://teens.drugabuse.gov/teachers (accessed 6 February 2020).

Additional resources include:

Glazzard, J and Bancroft, K (2018) *Meeting the Mental Health Needs of Learners 11–18 Years*. St Albans: Critical Publishing.

Glazzard, J and Mitchell, C (2018) *Social Media and Mental Health in Schools*. St Albans: Critical Publishing.

+CHAPTER 7

INTIMATE AND SEXUAL RELATIONSHIPS

CHAPTER OBJECTIVES

After reading this chapter you will understand:

+ the characteristics of healthy intimate relationships;

+ examples of how sexual pressure can be applied;

+ what to teach students in relation to contraception;

+ key myths and facts about pregnancy and miscarriage;

+ the requirements of the Abortion Act (1967) and the need to teach students about abortion;

+ the importance of teaching students about sexually transmitted infections;

+ the relationship between risk, sex and health.

INTRODUCTION

The statutory guidance states that the Relationships and Sex Education curriculum should give students the information that they need to establish and develop healthy and nurturing relationships. It also requires schools to teach students about the characteristics of healthy relationships and what makes a good friend, a good colleague and a successful marriage (or other type of committed relationship). In addition to this, the guidance states that schools should also teach students about intimate relationships, resisting pressure to have sex and not applying pressure, contraception, and what is acceptable and unacceptable behaviour in relationships. This chapter addresses these requirements and provides guidance to support your teaching of each topic. Throughout the chapter, case study material is provided to support your planning and to illuminate effective practice. Some critical questions are also asked to encourage you to reflect on your current understanding of the topics and issues that are discussed.

HEALTHY INTIMATE RELATIONSHIPS

It is important that students understand that healthy intimate relationships are underpinned by mutual respect, consent, loyalty, trust and sex. Students need to understand the principles of consent and the law relating to consent. Healthy intimate relationships are usually underpinned by friendship, shared interests and shared viewpoints. However, it is important that students recognise that intimate partners may sometimes have different interests and viewpoints but that mutual respect for different perspectives is always a characteristic of healthy relationships. Although friendship is often a characteristic of intimate relationships, this is not always the case. People can have healthy intimate relationships without establishing a friendship, but mutual respect and consent should always be evident within these relationships.

Young people live in a world where people have intimate relationships but where monogamy is not always upheld within these relationships. It is important that students recognise that this is not always a negative characteristic of those relationships, providing that both partners agree to this; for example, by agreeing to the principles of an open relationship. In addition, the increasing use of online dating platforms has made it easier for people to achieve intimacy with other people without necessarily establishing a 'traditional' relationship with the partners that they meet. Students need to understand that this is not necessarily negative, depending on one's beliefs, providing that the principles of consent and mutual respect are upheld within all types of relationships. Students should be supported to recognise that casual sexual relationships can be healthy, providing that they are aware of the risks involved, know how to protect themselves from these risks and that there is always consent and no sexual pressure, coercion or manipulation evident within these relationships.

CRITICAL QUESTIONS

+ What are your views on teaching students about casual intimate relationships?

+ What are the religious perspectives with regard to open relationships?

+ What are the religious perspectives in relation to casual sex?

+ Do you agree that students should be taught about casual intimacy, open relationships and other types of non-traditional relationships? Explain your views.

+ Do you agree that shared interests and shared views must be a characteristic of healthy intimate relationships? Justify your views.

SEXUAL PRESSURE

Sexual pressure can be applied through a variety of tactics. These include the following.

+ Coercion: using physical, psychological or emotional threats to make a person engage in sexual activity.

+ Manipulation: gaining agreement for sexual activity by increasing someone's vulnerability.

+ Exploitation: exploiting someone's vulnerability by offering support, shelter, food, money, alcohol or drugs in return for sexual activity.

If consent is sought through these tactics then it is assumed that consent has not been given and students need to recognise that sex without consent is illegal. Providing students with a range of scenarios for them to read and asking them to decide if sexual pressure has been applied or not is a useful way of supporting students to understand sexual pressure. Students also need to be taught a range of strategies for resisting sexual pressure. The statements below are useful for students to know:

+ *No thank you.*

+ *I don't want to.*

+ *I've changed my mind.*

+ *I need you to stop.*

(PSHE Association, 2015)

These statements are more effective than phrases where young people attempt to justify themselves in situations where they are exposed to sexual pressure. For example, '*I don't want to do this anymore because...*' invites the person applying the pressure to respond. It is far better to make a direct statement than to invite a response.

CONTRACEPTION

Students need to be taught about male and female contraception options. They need to understand that the purposes of contraception are to reduce the risk of unwanted pregnancy and the risk of contracting sexually transmitted infections. It is important to raise students' awareness of the importance of contraceptive use in reducing the risk of unintended pregnancy and sexually transmitted infections. Students need to know about hormonal and non-hormonal methods of contraception. Common hormonal methods include the contraceptive pill, implant, injection or patch. Common non-hormonal methods include the condom, femidom, diaphragm, intrauterine device and the use of spermicides. In addition, the rhythm method is often promoted by religious organisations that do not believe in contraception, although it can be unreliable.

Lessons on contraception should address:

+ *information about the different types of contraception, including emergency contraception;*

+ *the reasons for and benefits of abstaining from or delaying sexual activity;*

+ *information about the law as it relates to accessing contraception, where contraception can be accessed locally and the confidential nature of these services;*

+ *information about where and to whom to go to for [sic] confidential advice about contraception (including helplines and websites);*

+ *consideration of the advantages and disadvantages of the various types of contraception in terms of their effectiveness and the prevention of sexually transmitted infections;*

+ *discussion of combining different contraceptives, for example using the combined pill to prevent pregnancy and condoms to prevent sexually transmitted infections;*

+ *acknowledgement and discussion of the different religious views on contraception;*

+ *practising condom skills;*

+ *awareness of the impact of drinking and/or drug use on safe contraception.*

(www.cornwallhealthyschools.org/rse/sensitive-issues/contraception/, accessed 17 December 2019)

The national curriculum science content for Key Stage 3 states that students should be taught about reproduction in humans and the structure and function of the male and female reproductive systems. It also states that schools must teach students about the menstrual cycle (without details of hormones), gametes, fertilisation, gestation and birth and the effect of maternal lifestyle in the foetus through the placenta. When you are preparing to teach students about contraception, it is important that you consider what students have already been taught and how far they have progressed through the national curriculum science content. This will enable you to build upon students' prior knowledge and ensure that the sequencing of content is effectively planned across the school curriculum. You may also find it valuable to work with colleagues who have taught students about reproduction and to draw on their expertise to support your own planning and delivery.

When you are teaching students about contraception, it is also important to outline common myths. The myths that you discuss may include the following.

+ Long-term use of contraception can make it harder to get pregnant later in your life.

+ Emergency contraception is only effective the morning after unprotected sex.

+ Contraception is 100 per cent effective.

+ Hormonal contraceptives will increase the risk of cancer.

+ Hormonal contraceptives will cause you to gain weight.

+ All methods of contraception are appropriate for all women.

CASE STUDY

CONTRACEPTION

YEAR 9, SCIENCE

Students in Year 9 were taught a series of lessons on contraception. This topic was delivered once the students had finished learning about reproduction in their science lessons. The teacher with responsibility for teaching the students about contraception worked with the science teachers to identify how the topic could connect to students' prior learning. The science teachers outlined the areas of the content that they felt provided some overlap and they identified the specific points where the teacher could relate contraception to the content that had been delivered in earlier science lessons.

The sequence of lessons on contraception included:

+ teaching students about the role of contraception in relation to risk, pregnancy and sexually transmitted infections;

+ teaching students about the different types of contraception;

+ teaching students about the advantages and disadvantages of each type of contraception;

+ teaching students about emergency contraception and who can use it;

+ teaching students about the law in relation to contraception (including in relation to access and confidentiality);

+ teaching students about how to access support and advice in relation to contraception;

+ practising condom skills;

+ developing students' understanding of the impact of alcohol and drugs on the safe use of contraception.

CRITICAL QUESTIONS

+ How will you address religious perspectives on contraception?

+ What other potential issues might arise when teaching students about contraception and how will you address these?

PREGNANCY AND MISCARRIAGE

Students need to know key myths and facts about pregnancy. Myths include the following.

+ If your partner withdraws before he ejaculates, you won't get pregnant.

+ You cannot get pregnant during menstruation.

+ You cannot get pregnant if it is the first time you have sex.

+ You cannot get pregnant if you are breastfeeding.

+ Having one miscarriage means that you will have another.

+ Previous use of contraception will lead to a miscarriage.

+ It is a woman's fault when a miscarriage happens.

When you are teaching students about pregnancy and miscarriage, it is important to remember that your teaching needs to enable students to develop their prior knowledge. You should communicate with colleagues to identify what students have already been taught in relation to the national curriculum science content. This will enable you to sequence your curriculum and identify opportunities for students to make links to the content that they have been taught in other areas of the curriculum.

CRITICAL QUESTION

+ What potentially sensitive issues might arise when teaching students about miscarriage and how will you address these?

ABORTION

Students need to be taught the law in relation to abortion. The Abortion Act (1967) states that a registered medical practitioner may lawfully terminate a pregnancy providing that specific conditions are met. These are listed below.

+ The decision has to be approved by two doctors.

+ The pregnancy has not exceeded its 24th week.

+ The continuance of the pregnancy would involve risk, greater than if the pregnancy were terminated, of injury to the physical or mental health of the pregnant woman or any existing children of her family.

or:

+ The termination is necessary to prevent grave permanent injury to the physical or mental health of the pregnant woman.

or:

+ The continuance of the pregnancy would involve risk to the life of the pregnant woman, greater than if the pregnancy were terminated.

or:

+ There is a substantial risk that if the child were born it would suffer from physical or mental impairments.

Abortions after 24 weeks are allowed only if:

+ the woman's life is in danger;

+ there is a severe foetal abnormality;

+ the woman is at risk of grave physical and mental injury.

When you are teaching students about abortion, it is important to outline key facts. These include:

+ *abortion does not result in future infertility;*

+ *abortion does not increase the risk of miscarriage;*

+ *abortion does not increase the risk of developing breast cancer;*

+ *abortion does not cause mental illness;*

+ *current evidence suggests that the fetus is unable to feel pain under 24 weeks;*

+ *emergency contraception is not a method of abortion.*

(RCOG and FSRH, 2019)

Students should be taught to recognise and understand that an individual is entitled to their own views in relation to abortion. However, it is important that students are also aware of the law in terms of accessing an abortion and that is in an individual's legal right and decision to access an abortion as long as they meet the requirements to do so. If students discuss their views on abortion, they must understand that it is important to recognise other people's views and the requirements of the law.

CRITICAL QUESTIONS

+ How will you address religious perspectives on abortion?
+ What other potential and/or sensitive issues might arise when teaching students about abortion and how will you address these?

SEXUALLY TRANSMITTED INFECTIONS

Students need to be taught about common sexually transmitted infections (STIs), including syphilis, gonorrhoea, chlamydia, HIV and AIDS. They need to know how to protect themselves from risk of infection, the signs of infection and how to seek support if they have an infection. They also need to be taught to distinguish between myths and facts in relation to STIs.

Students need to know that some STIs can be treated and cured with antibiotic medicine, but that others cannot. Bacterial STIs are caused when bacteria are spread through vaginal, oral or anal sexual contact with an infected person. These infections include chlamydia, gonorrhoea and syphilis, and can generally be cured through antibiotic therapy.

Students also need to know that viral infections can be spread via the same routes as bacterial infections. However, they can also be spread through direct contact with infected skin or bodily fluids including blood, semen or saliva from an infected person entering into the bloodstream of an uninfected person. Viral infections include genital warts, hepatitis B, herpes and HIV, which are not curable, although the symptoms can be treated.

Students need to understand that although most STIs are generally transmitted through sexual encounters, some can be spread to others by sharing needles and syringes or through skin to skin contact, or are transferred from mother to unborn baby during pregnancy and child-birth. In addition, HIV can also be spread through breast milk.

Key facts include:

+ some STIs are bacterial and some are viral;

+ some STIs can be cured but some cannot be cured;

+ the majority of STIs have no symptoms or only mild symptoms;

+ in some cases, STIs can have serious reproductive health consequences;

+ each year, there are an estimated 376 million new infections.

Myths include:

+ people with STIs are dirty;

+ people with STIs are sexually promiscuous;

+ people cannot get STIs from oral sex;

+ only gay men and drug users can get HIV;

+ oral contraception can protect against STIs;

+ only people with multiple partners get STIs;

+ STIs will always go away without treatment.

RISKY SEXUAL BEHAVIOUR

Engaging in sexual activity with a person with a sexually transmitted infection increases the probability of receiving that infection. Sexual activity may also result in pregnancy or the pregnancy of the sexual partner. Students should be taught to recognise and understand these risks and that an individual's decisions may increase their exposure to these risks. It is also important to outline these risks within the context of rape and sexual abuse, and this is an opportunity to draw on linked concepts including consent and health.

SEX AND HEALTH

The choices that people make in relation to intimate relationships can affect all aspects of health. Physical, emotional and mental well-being can be affected by intimate relationships. If intimate relationships are unhealthy and involve coercion, manipulation and exploitation, this can have a detrimental impact on a person's emotional and mental health. These relationships can lead to depression, anxiety and other mental health conditions. They can also lead to low self esteem and lack of care for physical health. In contrast, healthy intimate relationships that are underpinned by mutual respect, consent, loyalty and trust can support individuals to be physically, emotionally and mentally healthy.

CASE STUDY

STUDENTS' PERSPECTIVES

ALL YEAR GROUPS, PSHE

This case study outlines research that was conducted by Rachel Heah as part of her PhD.

My PhD thesis aimed to examine the provision of Relationships and Sex Education (RSE) from a children's rights perspective. Between January and May 2018, focus groups were conducted with over 80 secondary school pupils from four participating secondary schools and one youth group in the Merseyside area of England. Pupils were asked about their experiences of school-based RSE lessons, in particular, what they liked and enjoyed about lessons, and what they felt needed to be changed or improved.

The young people in the study identified several aspects of the delivery of RSE in schools, particularly the following.

+ *'Professional' teachers.*
  - They wanted their teachers to be non-judgemental, and to create a positive environment for them to learn about RSE.
  - They wanted to be taught by 'professionals', ie, those who have relevant experience of teaching RSE, and, preferably, someone who has experience of relationships and sexual activity.

- They said that teachers should also have good knowledge of the topics being delivered, and maturity and confidence in delivering these topics. They should not be embarrassed or awkward when teaching RSE or when answering questions from pupils.
- Young people also preferred teachers who were closer in age to them, and of the same gender as them, as these teachers were seen to be more relatable. However, they appreciated that different teachers could offer different viewpoints.
- They valued being taught RSE by different teachers so that they have a wide variety of experiences to draw upon.

+ *Content and delivery of lessons.*

- Most young people interviewed requested more frequent RSE lessons (for example, once every few weeks, or once a month).
- They wanted schools to provide shorter and more spaced out lessons, rather than attempting to cram too much information into a lesson. They wanted enough time to process the information and ask necessary questions.
- In terms of content, young people valued lessons that offered real-world perspectives (or experiences) of the topics covered.
- Young people stated that they did not like it when their lessons were repetitive. This caused them to disengage.
- They also expressed dissatisfaction at lessons that were patronising or 'dumbed down'. For example, lessons involving the use of 'stick-men' drawings or 'pin-the-body-part' activities were seen as being particularly awkward.

+ *Opportunities to participate.*

- Young people also asked for the opportunity to be more involved with the development of the RSE curriculum. For example, some suggested that students should get to pick, via votes from a list, *who* comes into their school to give RSE lessons, and *what* is covered in those lessons.
- RSE lessons should offer young people the opportunity to ask questions and seek clarification without fear of judgement or punishment or without being told off for asking 'silly' questions.
- Several young people suggested introducing mechanisms, such as online polling or anonymous boxes, for them to ask questions anonymously during RSE lessons.

+ *Humour and fun in lessons.*

- Participants wanted their lessons to be more hands-on, interactive and engaging, perhaps through the use of games, activities and more visual aids, like images, pictures and videos. Lessons should be light-hearted and not overly serious. Introducing humour and laughter into RSE lessons was said to be a good way of reducing the embarrassment and awkwardness of discussing topics relating to sex.

(Heah, 2019)

SUMMARY

This chapter has explained the duty of schools to teach students about intimate relationships, contraception and abortion. It has also outlined key myths and facts on pregnancy, abortion and miscarriage and it has discussed the relationship between risk, sex and health. It has addressed key considerations in relation to each of these topics and it has provided guidance throughout to support your teaching. Within the chapter, case study material has been provided to support your planning and to illuminate effective practice. Some critical questions have also been asked to encourage you to reflect on your current understanding of the topics and issues that have been discussed.

FURTHER READING OR SOURCES OF FURTHER INFORMATION

The BBC has produced a teacher's pack, *Underage and Pregnant*, providing access to lesson plans, learning materials and short informative videos to support your teaching of some of the topics discussed in this chapter. This resource can be found at: www.ghll.org.uk/documents/Underage%20 Pregnancy.pdf (accessed 6 February 2020).

Additional resources include:

BBC Bitesize, *Sexual Health Class Clips*. [online] Available at: www.bbc.co.uk/ bitesize/topics/zqq2pv4/resources/2 (accessed 6 February 2020).

Royal College of Obstetricians and Gynaecologists (RCOG) and the Faculty of Sexual and Reproductive Healthcare (FSRH) (2019) *Abortion and Abortion Care Factsheet*. [online] Available at: www.pshe-association.org.uk/system/files/ fsrh-rcog-abortion-care-factsheet-rse-lessons%20%281%29.pdf (accessed 6 February 2020).

+CHAPTER 8

TEACHING RELATIONSHIPS AND SEX EDUCATION IN FAITH SCHOOLS

CHAPTER OBJECTIVES

After reading this chapter you will understand:

+ the implications of equality legislation;

+ religious perspectives on relationships (including marriage, monogamy and gender equality);

+ religious perspectives on sexuality, abortion and contraception.

INTRODUCTION

The DfE's subject content for religious studies states that GCSE specifications should develop students' knowledge and understanding of religious and non-religious beliefs. It also states that specifications should develop students' knowledge and understanding of religious beliefs and teachings as well as how religion influences individuals, communities and societies. The guidance also states that specifications must support students to understand significant common and divergent views between and/or within religions and beliefs. This chapter addresses many of these themes and as such it is important that you consider students' prior knowledge before you begin to deliver your own content. This will enable you to build upon students' prior knowledge and ensure that teaching is sequential across the school curriculum.

Within this chapter, the implications of equality legislation are outlined in relation to the teaching of Relationships and Sex Education. It also considers religious perspectives on relationships, sexuality, abortion and contraception. The chapter emphasises that it is important that your teaching is sensitive to the circumstances and experiences of the students that you are teaching and that all students are taught to respect the views of other people. As there is some overlap between this element of the statutory guidance and the required subject content in GCSE religious education specifications, you may also find it valuable to work with colleagues who have taught religious education to students and to draw on their expertise.

THE EQUALITY ACT (2010)

According to the RSE statutory guidance:

the religious background of all pupils must be taken into account when planning teaching, so that the topics that are included in the core content in this guidance are appropriately handled. Schools must ensure they comply with the relevant provisions of the Equality Act 2010, under which religion or belief are amongst the protected characteristics.

(DfE, 2019a, p 12)

93

In addition:

All schools may teach about faith perspectives. In particular, schools with a religious character may teach the distinctive faith perspective on relationships, and balanced debate may take place about issues that are seen as contentious. For example, the school may wish to reflect on faith teachings about certain topics as well as how their faith institutions may support people in matters of relationships and sex.

(DfE, 2019a, pp 12–13)

The Equality Act (2010) places a legal duty on schools to protect individuals with '*protected characteristics*' from direct and indirect discrimination and harassment. Protected characteristics include race, religion or belief, sexual orientation and gender reassignment. It is therefore crucial that students are taught to respect different religious perspectives on relationships, sexuality, abortion and contraception. In addition, it is also crucial that the perspectives and life choices of those with non-normative sexual orientations and gender identities are respected by everyone. Section 149 of the Equality Act places a Public Sector Equality Duty on schools, which requires schools to promote good relations between different groups of people. RSE therefore provides a unique context for students to learn about the views of people with different beliefs and the importance of respecting everyone's view regardless of one's personal perspective. Students should therefore be taught about the Equality Act (2010) and their own responsibilities in relation to it as well as the legal responsibilities of schools.

RELIGIOUS PERSPECTIVES ON RELATIONSHIPS

Different religions have different perspectives on relationships including perspectives on marriage, monogamy and gender hierarchy. A well-designed programme of RSE will introduce students to these perspectives. It will support students to debate different perspectives but also to demonstrate respect towards people with different beliefs. Different perspectives on these themes are summarised below.

MARRIAGE

+ Most Christians believe marriage is an important part of life. They believe the purpose of marriage is: to unite with someone they love for the rest of their lives; to be faithful and make this sacrament with God's blessing and in God's presence; and to have children who can also be part of the Christian faith. The Church of England does not regard homosexuality as a sin. However, it regards sex outside the confines of marriage as being sinful. Most Roman Catholics do not believe that homosexual feelings are a sin, but they do believe that the homosexual sex act is sinful. They do not agree with civil partnerships. Some Roman Catholics do not accept sex outside marriage, but some members of the Church of England may accept this if it leads to marriage.

+ In some religions (for example, Islam) marriage is a legal contract between a man and a woman.

+ Same-sex marriage is supported in some religions, for example, Sikhism, some denominations of Hinduism, Judaism and Christianity.

+ Same-sex marriage is not supported by Islam or the Catholic Church.

+ In Buddhism there is no official stance on same-sex marriage.

CRITICAL QUESTIONS

+ What are your personal perspectives in relation to same-sex marriage?

+ Why do you think perspectives on same-sex marriage might be changing?

MONOGAMY

Perspectives on monogamy vary according to religious belief or culture. Key terms for students to know are listed below.

+ Monogamy: this is a marriage consisting of only two parties.

+ Polygamy: this is when a man is married to more than one wife at a time.

+ Polyandry: this is when a woman is married to more than one husband at a time.

+ Bigamy: this is the practice of being married to two people at the same time and is illegal in most countries.

+ Group marriage: this is where three or more adults live together, all considering themselves partners, sharing finances children and household responsibilities.

+ Adultery: adultery is extramarital sex that is considered objectionable on social, religious, moral or legal grounds.

Different societies have different views on polygamy. Some predominantly Muslim countries accept polygamy and the practice is widespread in Africa.

CRITICAL QUESTIONS

+ How do perspectives on monogamy vary across different groups and societies?

+ What are your personal perspectives in relation to each of these practices?

GENDER HIERARCHY

The relationship between religion and gender equality is complex. Religion plays a crucially important role in shaping cultural, social, economic and political norms in many parts of the world. Gender roles and the status of women and men in society are linked to the manner in which religious texts have been interpreted for centuries. These texts have often been interpreted by people in positions of power and these have often been men. The interpretation of religious texts has resulted in gender inequality for many women for centuries. This has resulted in many women not achieving their full potential in many facets of their lives. Gender inequality has also resulted in men holding greater power than women in relationships, and in some cases it has resulted in women experiencing coercion, exploitation and manipulation and being denied their human rights. In some relationships, religious interpretations of texts have resulted in women experiencing domestic abuse.

Although attitudes towards gender equality may be changing within more liberal societies and groups, it is important to recognise that women still continue to experience inequalities not just because of religious perspectives but also because of institutional sexism, which is deeply engrained within many societies. For this reason, there continues to be a gender pay gap between males and females, and women continue to dominate the caring professions. Within the context of relationships women continue to be expected to look after the home and raise children, even within Western societies, although it is important to recognise that attitudes are slowly changing.

It is essential that students understand the difference between sex and gender. Sex is a biological construct that is assigned at birth. In contrast, gender is a socially constructed construct which is shaped by a process of socialisation. Individuals are socialised into gender roles from birth through a variety of influences including religion, families, communities, the media and educational contexts (Witt, 2000). Although perspectives on gender increasingly recognise gender as a fluid concept (Mavin and Grandy, 2012), within some relationships and within the context of some religions, traditional gender roles continue to be upheld (Woodhead, 2012).

CRITICAL QUESTIONS

+ How do perspectives on gender equality vary across religions?

+ How might you sensitively address these issues with students from different religious backgrounds?

CASE STUDY

RELIGION AND RELATIONSHIPS

YEAR 10, RELIGIOUS EDUCATION

Students in Year 10 were taught a sequence of lessons to outline religious perspectives on gender and sexuality. The sequence consisted of four lessons. Each of these lessons deconstructed and explored one overarching question. These were:

+ What does Christianity say about sexual relationships?

+ What does Christianity say about homosexuality?

+ What does Christianity say about marriage?

+ What does Christianity say about gender?

After the sequence, the students were given an opportunity to summarise the sequence, after which they then explored the same four questions within the context of another religion. During each lesson students were given an opportunity to discuss and debate legislation that related to the topic of discussion.

RELIGIOUS PERSPECTIVES ON SEXUALITY

Sex and religion are often considered uncomfortable bedfellows. It is interesting to note that people may share a religion but may have different perspectives on sexuality. In Islam, the Quran forbids homosexuality but UK Muslims generally have more progressive attitudes towards it. Perspectives in the Jewish faith can also vary although it is generally considered that homosexuality is contrary to orthodox Jewish teachings. Within the Sikh faith, there are no specific teachings about sexuality and same-sex relationships are permitted. The perspectives of Hindus vary. Some Hindus believe that homosexuality is a normal expression of human desires, and that homosexuality should be embraced. However, there are several Hindu groups that believe homosexuality is wrong. Perspectives also vary across those who follow the teachings of the Church of England. In addition, although the Catholic faith considers homosexuality to be a sin, it is possible to be homosexual and Catholic, providing that the individual does not act on their orientation.

Given these varied perspectives within each religion, it is important that students do not form stereotypes. Within modern society, people follow specific religions but also hold liberal views in relation to sexuality.

RELIGIOUS PERSPECTIVES ON ABORTION

It is important that students understand different religious perspectives on abortion and that they learn to respect different perspectives even though they may not agree with them. It is also important to remember that some students in the class may follow these religions so this topic needs to be addressed sensitively. From the outset, students need to understand that this is an emotive topic and people often have strong viewpoints in relation to it. Viewpoints may differ across individuals, and between groups and societies, but regardless, people's views still need to be respected.

Abortions must be carried out in a National Health Service (NHS) hospital, NHS agency or private premises approved by the Secretary of State for Health. A woman can have an abortion or termination of pregnancy if two doctors decide, '*in good faith*', that one or more of the grounds specified in the Abortion Act (1967) are met. These have been covered in Chapter 7.

All the religions have taken strong positions on abortion. These are summarised below.

+ Traditional Buddhism rejects abortion because it involves the deliberate destroying of a life. Modern Buddhists, however, are more divided about the morality of abortion. Buddhists regard life as starting at conception.

+ The Church of England combines strong opposition to abortion with a recognition that there can be, strictly limited, conditions under which it may be morally acceptable to abort.

+ The Roman Catholic Church says that deliberately causing an abortion is gravely morally wrong.

+ Hinduism is generally opposed to abortion except where it is necessary to save the mother's life.

+ Muslims regard abortion as wrong but many accept that it may be permitted if the continuation of the pregnancy would put the mother's life in danger.

+ Judaism does not forbid abortion, but it does not permit abortion on demand. Abortion is only permitted for serious reasons.

+ In Sikhism abortion is generally forbidden although the practice is not uncommon in the Sikh community due to a cultural preference for males.

Regardless of beliefs on abortion, students need to know the facts and myths about abortion. Key myths are identified below.

+ *Abortion does not result in future infertility. Fertility returns immediately after abortion.*

+ *Abortion does not increase the risk of miscarriage, ectopic pregnancy or a low placenta in future pregnancies. There may be a slightly higher risk of future premature birth but the risk is very low.*

+ Abortion does not increase the risk of developing breast cancer.

+ Abortion does not cause mental illness.

+ Current evidence suggests that the fetus is unable to feel pain under 24 weeks.

+ Emergency contraception, taken after unprotected sex, is not a method of abortion. Pregnancy only starts when a fertilised egg implants in the wall of the womb.

(RCOG and FSRH, 2019)

CRITICAL QUESTIONS

+ How might you address different religious perspectives on abortion within the student body?

+ What is your perspective on abortion and why?

RELIGIOUS PERSPECTIVES ON CONTRACEPTION

Students need to understand that perspectives on contraception may vary according to religious belief. These are summarised below.

+ Most Buddhists believe that conception occurs when an egg is fertilised, so contraception that prevents fertilisation is not usually objected to, although the views of individual Buddhists may vary.

+ In the Church of England, contraception is not regarded as a sin or going against God's purpose.

+ The Catholic Church has been opposed to contraception since at least the second century.

+ Hindus believe that all methods of contraception are permitted.

+ In Islam all forms of contraception are acceptable in special circumstances. These are usually to do with protecting the life of the mother or preventing a pregnancy if the woman is breastfeeding.

+ Within liberal Jewish perspectives it is generally agreed that women may use contraception as long as it is one of the forms that means

100

that sexual intercourse can occur naturally and without any barrier; for example, by using the contraceptive pill.

+ In Sikhism the use of contraception is acceptable and it is up to a couple to decide whether and when to use it.

The emphasis should be on supporting students to respect different beliefs regardless of their own personal perspective on contraception.

CRITICAL QUESTIONS

+ How might you address different religious perspectives on contraception within the student body?

+ What is your perspective on contraception and why?

CASE STUDY

CONTRACEPTION

YEAR 10, PSHE

Year 10 students took part in a range of activities to support and develop their understanding of contraceptive methods. To begin the lesson, the teacher provided some statistics relating to contraception and she explained that students would be learning about contraceptive methods. After this initial discussion, the teacher then led students through a range of tasks and discussions. The lesson included:

+ asking students to state the methods of contraception that they already knew about;

+ collecting these ideas and adding them to a class whiteboard, after which the teacher added any additional ideas (so that the list included the full range of methods she wanted to discuss during the lesson);

+ identifying (by circling on the whiteboard) the methods that are most used by young people and explaining that the lesson would focus on these methods;

+ splitting the class into groups and assigning one contraceptive method to each group;

+ providing each group with a fact sheet about the contraceptive method that they had been assigned;

+ asking each group to prepare a three-minute presentation which addressed the following questions:

  - Does the method guarantee 100 per cent protection from sexually transmitted infections?
  - Does the method prevent all chance of pregnancy?
  - How effective is the method?
  - Where can you access or purchase the method?

+ telling all students that during each presentation there is an expectation to collect and record information if you are not in the presenting group.

(adapted from an original resource by www.advocatesforyouth.org, accessed 17 December 2019)

SUMMARY

This chapter has outlined the implications of equality legislation in relation to the teaching of Relationships and Sex Education. It has considered religious perspectives on relationships and it has also discussed marriage, monogamy and gender equality within this context. Guidance has been provided to support your understanding of each and to support you to teach students about these concepts and perspectives. The chapter has outlined religious perspectives in relation to sexuality, abortion and contraception. We have emphasised that it is important that students are taught to recognise a range of religious perspectives and that it is essential to respect people's individual views on these. Throughout the chapter we have also emphasised that it is important to remember that some of the students in your care may follow the religions that you are discussing, and that teaching must be sensitive to this. Case study material has been offered throughout to illuminate effective practice and critical questions have been asked to support your reflection.

FURTHER READING OR SOURCES OF FURTHER INFORMATION

The Catholic Education Service has published lesson resources to support the delivery of Relationships and Sex Education. These resources include model policies, best practice, governance audits and case studies. The materials are available at: http://catholiceducation.org.uk/schools/relationship-sex-education (accessed 6 February 2020).

Childnet.com has published similar guidance and provides some focus on the implications of the statutory guidance for faith schools. Their guidance is available at: www.childnet.com/ufiles/RSE-guidance-including-faith-schools-and-handling-sensitive-topics.pdf (accessed 6 February 2020).

The PSHE Association's PSHE Education Programme of Study (Key Stages 1–5) provides guidance on the teaching of the topics in this chapter. Their programme is available at: www.pshe-association.org.uk/system/files/PSHE%20Education%20Programme%20of%20Study%20%28Key%20stage%201–5%29%20Jan%202017_2.pdf (accessed 6 February 2020).

The contraception case study in this chapter was originally adapted from a lesson plan that was published by Advocates for Youth (www.advocatesforyouth.org). This resource can be accessed at: www.advocatesforyouth.org/wp-content/uploads/storage//advfy/lesson-plans/lesson-plan-contraception-part-i-and-ii.pdf (accessed 6 February 2020).

+CHAPTER 9

WORKING IN PARTNERSHIP WITH PARENTS AND EXTERNAL AGENCIES

CHAPTER OBJECTIVES

After reading this chapter you will understand:

+ ways of working in partnership with parents;

+ the role of external organisations in supporting RSE delivery;

+ how to address potential challenges.

INTRODUCTION

This chapter outlines some of the potential challenges associated with RSE delivery. It outlines some of the controversial aspects of RSE content that parents might object to and provides a strategy for consulting with parents. The chapter also highlights the valuable contribution that external organisations can make to RSE delivery, including the police, health services and community organisations. RSE curriculum content is so broad that it might not be possible for a teacher to be an expert in all aspects of that subject content. Organisations which have first-hand experiences of addressing aspects of that content can support delivery, thus enhancing the richness of the curriculum. Finally, the chapter outlines the importance of working in partnership with social care services.

POTENTIAL CHALLENGES

Some parents might object to schools teaching students about Sex Education because they believe that as parents they retain the right to support their child's understanding of sex. In addition, some parents might object to their child learning about LGBT identities, same-sex marriage and same-sex relationships. It is possible that these identities and relationships conflict with their personal or religious values. Parents retain the right to withdraw their child from Sex Education only. They are not entitled to withdraw their child from Relationships Education and schools are required to deliver the statutory content in the guidance. This includes learning about different types of relationships. Therefore, schools will need to consider carefully how to develop a process of consultation with parents so that parents understand what is being taught, when it is being taught and how it is being taught. Schools that can demonstrate that they have consulted with parents will receive the backing of the Department for Education in relation to parental challenges.

PARENTAL RIGHT TO WITHDRAW

The statutory guidance provides parents with the right to withdraw their child from the Sex Education component of the RSE curriculum but not the Relationships or Health Education components. Key facts are stated below.

+ Parents will not be able to withdraw their child from any aspect of Relationships Education or Health Education.

+ Parents will be able to withdraw their child, following discussion with the school, from any or all aspects of Sex Education, other than those which are part of the science curriculum, up to and until three terms before the age of 16.

+ After the age of 16, the guidance states that '*if the child wishes to receive sex education rather than be withdrawn, the school should make arrangements to provide the child with sex education during one of those terms*'.

+ Where students are withdrawn from Sex Education, schools should record the process and will have to '*ensure that the student receives appropriate, purposeful education during the period of withdrawal*'.

CRITICAL QUESTIONS

+ Should parents have the right to withdraw their children from Sex Education? Justify your views.

+ Why might parents object to aspects of RSE content?

+ Is it the role of schools or parents to teach Sex Education? Justify your views.

DEVELOPING CONSULTATION WITH PARENTS

Developing a process of consultation with parents is not a single event. It should be a process that takes place over time. However, parents do not hold the right to veto curriculum content. Ways of developing a process of consultation are outlined below.

+ *Hold a briefing event.*

  – Hold a briefing event for parents to outline the school's approach to the RSE curriculum.
  – Ensure that parents know what is being taught, when it is being taught and how it is being taught.
  – Show parents examples of the resources that will be used to support lesson delivery.

106

- Ensure that parents understand the school's legal obligations in relation to the Equality Act (2010).
- Highlight some of the possible tensions between religion and sex and relationships and explain to parents how these will be mediated to ensure that everyone's views are respected.

+ *Develop a working group.*

- Invite some parents to form a working group that includes staff and governors to support the development of the school's approach to RSE.
- The role of the working group might be to develop a vision and a curriculum plan that outlines when aspects of subject content will be taught.

+ *Consult widely.*

- Provide parents with an opportunity to share their views on the school's approach to the RSE curriculum via an online survey.

+ *Keep parents informed.*

- Communicate regularly with parents about RSE curriculum delivery through blogs, newsletters and the school website.
- Provide parents with fact sheets so that they can support the school's curriculum programme at home.
- Provide guidance to parents on how to address difficult, awkward or sensitive questions from their child at home.

WORKING WITH HEALTH CARE SERVICES

Health care services in the community, such as the local NHS Trust, may be willing to support aspects of curriculum delivery. Health care services are well-placed to deliver aspects of the Health Education component, including the risks associated with tobacco, drugs and alcohol, and ways of breaking addiction. Health care services are also experienced in delivering content about mental well-being and will be able to ensure that students receive accurate and up-to-date information about different forms of mental ill-health and ways of looking after one's own mental health. In addition, health care services have excellent knowledge about aspects of Sex Education, including contraception, abortion and sexually transmitted infections.

Schools should therefore identify aspects of curriculum content that might be enhanced by working in partnership with local health care services. Involving health professionals in curriculum delivery will help to make the programme richer and support students' engagement with the curriculum content.

CRITICAL QUESTIONS

+ How might cutbacks to services in recent years impact on partnership working with health care services?

+ How might schools address this problem?

WORKING WITH THE POLICE

The police have excellent knowledge of the law. They are well-placed to support curriculum delivery in relation to the law. The police can provide information about the law in relation to a variety of topics including substance misuse, domestic abuse and sexual crimes. They are also well-placed to provide information to students on the law relating to sharing explicit images, consent and hate crime.

Police services have special units that deal specifically with domestic abuse. Police officers are trained to recognise different forms of domestic abuse. They are also trained in the characteristics of perpetrators and they have a specialist understanding of how domestic abuse starts and how it progresses. They work with perpetrators and victims daily and therefore have both a theoretical and working knowledge of this issue. Their involvement in this aspect of curriculum delivery would make an excellent contribution to the programme design.

In addition, the police work daily with a wide range of criminals, including extremists, terrorists, abusers, people with substance dependency and fraudsters. They understand how criminal behaviour starts and how it progresses. They work in partnership with a wide range of families and communities and therefore with people from different backgrounds and beliefs. They have front-line experience of many of the aspects of subject content in the RSE guidance. The police service is a rich resource that schools should draw upon to support the programme. Services provide an education division which will liaise and work with schools to ensure that young people receive accurate and up-to-date information.

CRITICAL QUESTIONS

+ How might cutbacks to services in recent years impact on partnership working with the police?

+ How might schools address this problem?

+ What are the advantages of working in partnership with the police?

+ What are the associated challenges?

CASE STUDY

WORKING IN PARTNERSHIP WITH THE POLICE

YEAR 10, PSHE

A school designed a sequence of lessons to teach students about domestic abuse. These are outlined below.

Lesson 1

Students were taught about what domestic abuse is and different types of domestic abuse, including emotional, psychological and physical abuse.

Lesson 2

The local police unit came into school to talk to the students about how domestic abuse starts and how it progresses. Students were taught the signs to help them identify domestic abuse within relationships and they were taught how to seek support.

Lesson 3

A female survivor of domestic abuse came into school to share her experiences of domestic abuse with the students, including the impact of domestic abuse on her life. The students had an opportunity to ask questions.

Lesson 4

A former perpetrator of domestic abuse (from a same-sex relationship) came into school to talk to the students about his motivations for carrying out abuse, the types of abuse he subjected his partner to and how he sought help for his problems. Students were given an opportunity to ask him questions.

CRITICAL QUESTIONS

+ What are the ethical considerations that the school must address in relation to these four lessons?
+ What sensitive issues might arise in the classroom when addressing domestic abuse?
+ How might you address these?

WORKING IN PARTNERSHIP WITH COMMUNITY ORGANISATIONS

A wide range of community organisations can support RSE delivery. These include local charities, the fire and rescue service, local sports organisations and even companies such as banks. A variety of local charities exist to support Health and Sex Education; for example, charities that provide sexual advice for people from the LGBT community. Many football clubs and other sports organisations are passionate about working in partnership with schools to support students' understanding of mental health and physical health. Services in the community for elderly people provide valuable opportunities for students to gain experience of volunteering, which will support the development of positive character virtues. Many large companies are committed to a social justice agenda as well as a financial agenda and are therefore very willing to work in partnership with schools, colleges and universities to support aspects of education.

CRITICAL QUESTIONS

+ What are the advantages of working in partnership with community organisations?

+ What other community organisations might support RSE delivery?

CASE STUDY

WORKING IN PARTNERSHIP WITH RELIGIOUS ORGANISATIONS

YEAR 11, RELIGIOUS EDUCATION

A school designed a sequence of lessons to cover different religious perspectives on relationships and sex. A representative from the faith was invited into school to lead each lesson. Each lesson covered:

+ the faith perspective on marriage, including monogamy and polygamy;

+ the faith perspective on same-sex relationships and same-sex marriage;

+ the faith perspective on abortion;

+ the faith perspective on contraception.

Each lesson covered a different religion and the Roman Catholic faith and teachings of the Church of England were addressed in separate lessons. Following a presentation, students were provided with an opportunity to ask the faith representative questions and engage in debate.

WORKING WITH SOCIAL CARE SERVICES

The RSE curriculum covers a range of sensitive topics including, but not limited to, consent, rape, grooming, sexual abuse, emotional and physical abuse and online abuse. It is possible that students may wish to make a disclosure to the teacher which immediately triggers a safeguarding concern given the nature of the content that is being discussed. It might be through participation in lessons that young people who have been exposed to abuse begin to recognise for the first time that the abuse they have been exposed to is illegal. Schools should treat all disclosures extremely seriously and follow the guidance in the document *Keeping Children Safe in Education: Statutory Guidance for Schools and Colleges* (DfE, 2019c). Assurances of confidentiality should not be made and teachers should report concerns to the designated safeguarding lead (DSL). Schools should refer specific cases to social care services.

SUMMARY

This chapter has outlined ways of working in partnership with parents through a programme of consultation to support RSE delivery. It has outlined ways of working in partnership with the police, health services and community organisations to support RSE curriculum delivery. Given the breadth of subject content, it is important that teachers who deliver RSE are adequately trained and prepared for their roles. Enhancing initial teacher training curriculum content and professional development for serving teachers will be critical to ensure that teachers feel confident in delivering that content. Schools will need to ensure that the teachers who are deployed to teach RSE are confident, knowledgeable and enthusiastic so that students receive their entitlement to a high-quality curriculum. In addition, schools should ensure that there is adequate curriculum time allocated to this subject and that there is a well-sequenced curriculum plan that supports the development of students' knowledge and skills over time so that there is progression but also so that content is delivered at the right time.

FURTHER READING OR SOURCES OF FURTHER INFORMATION

PSHE Association. Available at: www.pshe-association.org.uk/ (accessed 6 February 2020).

PSHE Association Guidance on Working in Partnership with Parents. Available at: www.pshe-association.org.uk/curriculum-and-resources/resources/relationships-education-and-rse-guides-supporting (accessed 6 February 2020).

Sex Education Forum. Available at: www.sexeducationforum.org.uk/ (accessed 6 February 2020).

+CHAPTER 10

RSE FOR STUDENTS WITH SPECIAL EDUCATIONAL NEEDS AND DISABILITIES

CHAPTER OBJECTIVES

After reading this chapter you will understand:

+ the legal obligations that schools must meet in relation to young people with disabilities;

+ how to support students with Special Educational Needs and Disabilities (SEND) to establish and develop relationships;

+ the need to support students with SEND to learn about intimate relationships.

INTRODUCTION

Young people of the same age might be developmentally at different stages. Teaching methods should therefore consider young people's different needs, particularly in relation to those with Special Educational Needs and Disabilities (SEND). The statutory guidance for Relationships Education (DfE, 2019a) advises schools to consider these needs by adopting flexible modes of delivery. Some young people may need a specific programme which is tailored to meet their needs, some delivery might take place in small groups and some delivery might take place with the whole class. This chapter addresses the relationship education needs of young people with SEND.

LEGISLATION

The Equality Act (2010) sets out the legal obligations that schools must meet in relation to young people with disabilities. The legal main duties of schools are listed below.

+ Schools must not directly or indirectly discriminate against, harass or victimise disabled young people.

+ Schools must make reasonable adjustments to ensure that young people with disabilities are not at a substantial disadvantage compared with their peers.

+ The Public Sector Equality Duty states that schools must foster good relations between young people who have a disability and those who do not.

Schools must therefore ensure that young people with SEND receive their entitlement to a Relationships Education curriculum. Schools must ensure that students with disabilities are supported to establish healthy relationships. This will help to ensure that young people with SEND are not subjected to discrimination. They have the same right to enjoy relationships as all young people do. If they do not have the necessary skills required to establish healthy relationships, the Relationships Education curriculum should support them to develop these skills so that they can experience the benefits of relationships. A tailored curriculum that focuses on developing relationship skills might constitute a reasonable adjustment in relation to the equality legislation.

COMMUNICATION AND INTERACTION NEEDS

Some learners with SEND have specific difficulties with establishing relationships. Students with speech, language and communication needs, including those who stammer, are particularly vulnerable to being bullied because of their difficulties. They may develop low self esteem, and this can impact on their ability to form relationships with others. As a result of low self esteem, they may not develop self respect, which is critical for relationship building. They may also lack confidence in seeking relationships because of their language and communication difficulties. Developing self esteem and understanding of self respect are essential so that young people with communication and interaction needs can build healthy relationships. In addition, other students may need support in understanding how to communicate with peers who have communication and interaction needs, including the importance of demonstrating respect and patience towards those with communication difficulties.

Students who are identified with Autistic Spectrum Conditions (ASC) typically have three main areas of difficulty which can impact on their ability to form relationships. They often experience difficulties with social interaction, social communication and rigidity of thought.

Students with ASC may find social interaction difficult. Some will find it difficult to work with others in pairs and small groups and this can make it difficult for them to establish relationships. It is important to recognise that students with ASC are individuals. Some will have greater capacity for social interaction than others and some will find any social interaction distressing. Difficulties with social communication may mean that young people with ASC might struggle to understand the rules of social communication. They might experience difficulty with maintaining eye contact and with turn-taking and the use of non-verbal cues to support verbal interactions. In addition, they might struggle to understand the 'backwards and forwards' nature of communication. Fundamentally, the key area of difficulty lies with communication rather than language. Difficulties in social communication can mean that young people with autism struggle to establish relationships. Rigid thought processes can be evident, which often result in a desire for consistency and clear routines. When routines change, this can result in distress, which can impact on their behaviour. Peers need to understand the potential triggers for specific behaviours and respond to them with patience and empathy.

116

In addition to these key areas of difficulty, young people with autism may struggle to demonstrate empathy towards others. They lack a theory of mind. Essentially, this means that they may fail to respond to others with empathy when people are distressed. They may also make inappropriate but literal comments about others because they might not understand how their words and actions can impact on other people. Difficulties with demonstrating empathy towards others can affect their capacity to form relationships with peers, particularly if they demonstrate socially inappropriate behaviour.

CRITICAL QUESTIONS

+ Is the guidance in the statutory guidance for Relationships Education adequate to support teachers to provide Relationships Education for young people with SEND?

+ How can schools best provide Relationships Education for young people with SEND?

CASE STUDY

RELATIONSHIPS EDUCATION FOR YOUNG PEOPLE WITH AUTISM

YEAR 8, PSHE

Students with autism were being taught about Relationships and Sex Education and their teacher took steps to ensure that the teaching was responsive to their needs. The teacher met with the parents of all students to discuss the sequence of lessons and to provide an opportunity for parents to share concerns about how their child may respond.

Some parents felt that their children did not need to attend the lessons as they did not feel comfortable in social situations and as such were not vulnerable. In response to this the teacher highlighted some statistics and facts in relation to sexual abuse. This information showed the number of reports of sexual abuse against adults with disabilities and the proportion of these reports that involved learning disabilities. The teacher also explained that some students with additional needs were more dependent on others to meet their personal care needs and that this meant that students had to be taught about Relationships and Sex Education.

A different parent explained that they did not have any queries in relation to the content of the lesson but that they were concerned about their child's ability to deal with the concepts being discussed. The teacher explained that the lesson would take place in a normal classroom environment and that students would be told about what the lesson was going to involve before it took place. The teacher also explained that she would have one-to-one conversations with all students prior to the lessons to inform students that they did not need to actively participate in any activities. She used this as an opportunity to invite students to agree particular roles in relation to any input they may wish to have during the lesson. The teacher explained to the parent that this would reduce possible anxiety.

COGNITION AND LEARNING NEEDS

Students with cognition and learning needs form a diverse group. Needs may range from moderate learning difficulties (MLDs) to profound and multiple learning difficulties (PMLDs). Some young people may also have specific learning difficulties such as dyslexia, dyscalculia and dyspraxia (SpLDs).

It is important to consider carefully the needs of young people within this group. Some students with cognition and learning needs may be operating at an earlier stage of cognitive development than the majority of their peers of the same age. The Relationships Education curriculum for these students will therefore need to be age appropriate.

Young people with cognition and learning needs are vulnerable to exploitation within relationships. The curriculum should therefore help them to recognise when relationships are making them feel unhappy or unsafe. They need to be taught to recognise coercion, manipulation and other forms of abuse so that they can identify these if they occur. In addition, they also need to know how to report their concerns to other people, how to access support and who to talk to if they feel that they are being abused.

Some students with cognition and learning needs will have low self esteem. Their view of themselves (self concept) will be informed by the views that others have of them including peers and adults. If other people demonstrate negative views towards them, they may start to internalise these views and develop a poor self concept. Their self esteem is also influenced by their self efficacy. Self efficacy is their perception of their own competence. As a result of their cognition and learning needs, there is a risk that they may start to develop a negative view of their own competence. This will impact negatively on their self esteem. If they start to develop low self esteem there is also a risk that they will not develop self respect. They may start to feel that they are not a good enough person and therefore not worthy of other people's respect. Therefore, it is essential that young people learn through the Relationships Education curriculum that they are worthy of self respect and that they have a right to expect this from others. A well-designed Relationships Education curriculum for students with cognition and learning needs should therefore focus on developing their self esteem and their understanding of self respect. As their self esteem develops, this should support them in recognising that they have a right to self respect, although self respect may need to be explicitly taught.

Young people with cognition and learning needs may also need to learn that their body belongs to them and that other people should not touch their body without permission. As they may be vulnerable to abuse, it is critical that they understand that other people are not entitled to invade their personal space or touch their body without their permission. Additionally, it is critical for them to understand that they should not touch other people's bodies without permission and that they should not invade other people's personal space. Some young people with cognition and learning needs will seek other people's affection physic-ally by touching other people. These students need to understand that although some forms of touch are acceptable, other forms of touch are unacceptable and they may therefore need to be taught about more appropriate ways of greeting people. A simple example is to teach them to greet others using a handshake rather than a hug. This prevents them from invading other people's personal space and also minimises the risk that they might be abused.

Students with cognition and learning needs may find it difficult to develop relationships with others. A range of factors contribute to this, including the fact that they might be operating at an earlier stage of cognitive development than their same-age peers. The character traits that support people to effectively build relationships may also need to explicitly be taught through modelling. These include truthfulness, trust, loyalty, kindness, generosity, respect, courtesy and manners. Young people with cognition and learning needs may need a carefully designed structured programme of character education that systematically

119

enables them to learn about these important character traits which will help them to establish secure, healthy relationships.

Students with mild and specific learning difficulties may also experience difficulties establishing secure relationships due to low self esteem and low confidence. Students of the same age may be developmentally at different stages and this can impact on their readiness for Relationships Education.

SOCIAL, EMOTIONAL AND MENTAL HEALTH NEEDS

Students with social, emotional and mental health needs are a diverse group, which includes young people with behavioural needs but also those with more specific mental health needs. Students with social, emotional and mental health needs may also find it difficult to establish relationships. Peers may interpret their behaviour as negative and socially undesirable and they may choose not to interact with them. Students' unmet needs are often reflected through their behaviours. Many young people with poor behaviour have experienced trauma, parental conflict, abuse and neglect. Often their basic needs are not met and they may have poor self esteem. Their difficulties may arise from not forming secure early attachments. Young people living in areas of social deprivation are more likely to experience mental ill-health, and young people who are looked after or those who identify as LGBT are more at risk of developing mental ill-health.

Behaviour is usually an attempt by the student to communicate an unmet need. They may demonstrate specific undesirable behaviours for a range of complex reasons and these behaviours can detrimentally impact on their ability to establish healthy relationships with others. Unacceptable behaviour can originate from low self esteem, poor attachment, experience of abuse, neglect, rejection and trauma. In addition, some unacceptable behaviours may have been modelled in the family or community contexts. Young people with social, emotional and mental health needs may struggle to establish relationships because they may have experienced, or be experiencing, unhealthy relationships in their families and communities. They may have been let down by others in relationships and they might not trust other people. Some students may also be reluctant to establish relationships with them due to their complex needs. They may need a tailored Relationships Education curriculum through which they learn:

120

+ the value of healthy human relationships;

+ the character traits that will support them in establishing healthy relationships;

+ emotional literacy and regulation skills;

+ social behaviour and regulation skills;

+ self respect;

+ how others can be a source of support;

+ how to seek help if relationships are unhealthy;

+ to develop their self esteem.

Mental health needs may arise from young people's experiences of unhealthy relationships. These negative experiences may have led them to believe that unhealthy relationships are typical of all relationships and that they do not deserve self respect. Through Relationships Education, young people can start to understand the differences between healthy and unhealthy relationships. They can start to understand that they deserve respect from others, and they can learn how to report abuse when they experience it. As students learn about the characteristics of unhealthy relationships, they may have to reframe their previous understanding of relationships, particularly if they have been exposed to unhealthy relationships in other contexts. Young people's social backgrounds should not define what they become. Through the Relationships Education curriculum, young people can learn to critically evaluate the previous relationships to which they have been exposed, particularly if those relationships have been unhealthy and resulted in them developing social, emotional and mental health needs.

CASE STUDY

RELATIONSHIPS EDUCATION FOR YOUNG PEOPLE WITH COMMUNICATION AND INTERACTION NEEDS

YEAR 7, PSHE

Students with autism in a secondary school were taught the skills of emotional and social regulation. They struggled to understand the rules of social communication and they could not interpret other people's feelings. They participated in an intervention programme which helped them to learn the rules of social communication. This included the skills of turn-taking, the use of gesture and when to take pauses in conversation. They also learned about a range of feelings and how to regulate their feelings. This intervention helped them to establish more effective relationships with their peers.

SENSORY NEEDS

Sensory needs include visual impairment, hearing impairment and multisensory impairment. The complex needs of these students may mean that they develop low self esteem, which can detrimentally impact on their ability to form relationships with others. Their needs can also prevent peers from establishing relationships with them. A key aim of Relationships Education is for young people to learn to respect people's differences. Young people with sensory needs may need a tailored pro-gramme through which they learn to develop their self esteem and their understanding of self respect. Strategies to support young people with sensory impairment for building relationships are listed below:

+ introduce a programme to develop self esteem;

+ teach about the importance of self respect;

+ teach all young people strategies to facilitate communication with young people with sensory needs, including sign language;

+ teach all young people about the importance of respecting others irrespective of differences;

+ provide young people with a sensory need with a 'buddy' who can support them, particularly during unstructured time;

+ teach all young people to assess risk particularly for young people with visual impairment who may be at risk of injury.

PHYSICAL NEEDS

Students with physical needs may need specific support in developing relationships. Their physical needs may mean that they have restricted mobility and they may therefore not have the same agility as their peers. They may find it more challenging to participate in some of the activities that their peers undertake and they may have developed low self esteem as a result of their needs. It is therefore important, first and foremost, to focus on developing their self esteem so that they are more confident in establishing relationships with others. It is also important to teach all students to respect people's differences and to suggest ways that they can include young people with physical needs into their activities. Developing social connectivity is vital for good mental health and the Relationships Education should therefore be designed to support all young people to develop healthy friendships.

Some young people with physical needs may be vulnerable to bullying. A well-designed Relationships Education curriculum should therefore ensure that all students can identify the characteristics of unhealthy relationships and that they know how to report their concerns to others. All students need to be taught to recognise bullying within relationships so that they can act if this occurs.

It is also possible that young people with physical needs have been protected from danger within the context of their families and communities. However, all young people need to be encouraged to take safe risks. They need to be able to identify and manage risks so that they can experience equality of opportunity. Risk will be presented within the context of friendships, particularly when young people with physical needs participate in activities with other young people. All young people therefore need to understand the concepts of safe and unsafe risks within relationships. It might be extremely dangerous for a student with physical needs to participate in specific activities, but students should be taught how to adapt activities to ensure that all young people can participate safely.

Some young people with physical needs may not have experience of developing relationships with their peers due to parental concerns about their safety. They might not have experienced the same opportunities to meet other young people socially outside school and they might not participate in co-curricular activities, particularly if their parents are concerned that specific activities may present risks. A well-rounded education supports young people to develop social relationships. Social relationships improve overall well-being and foster a sense of belonging within school. Young people who have less experience of establishing relationships may therefore need additional support in developing their social and emotional literacy and regulatory skills so that they can form healthy relationships with others. In addition, they may benefit from a structured programme which systematically introduces them to positive character traits that should be demonstrated within the context of relationships.

TEACHING SEND STUDENTS ABOUT INTIMATE RELATIONSHIPS

Some students with autism will be operating at an earlier stage of cognitive development. However, they have a right to intimate relationships when they feel ready. Developing their emotional and social literacy will help them to establish loving and trusting relationships. They need to be supported to develop empathy and social communication skills so that they can establish healthy relationships. In addition, they need to understand about a range of issues in relationships including risk, exploitation, coercion and manipulation. They need to understand about the characteristics of healthy relationships and the importance of consent within intimate relationships.

SUMMARY

This chapter has emphasised that young people of the same age might be developmentally at different stages. It has therefore outlined the importance of ensuring that teaching methods consider students' different needs, particularly in relation to those with Special Educational Needs and Disabilities (SEND). It has highlighted the requirements of the statutory guidance for Relationships Education in relation to these needs and it has explained the benefits of employing flexible modes of delivery. The chapter has also explained that some students may need a specific programme which is tailored to meet their needs and that some delivery might take place in small groups and some delivery might take place with the whole class. Case study material has been offered to illuminate effective practice and critical questions have been asked to support your reflection.

FURTHER READING OR SOURCES OF FURTHER INFORMATION

Big Talk Education has published frequently asked questions that relate to Relationships and Sex Education for parents of children on the autism spectrum. It is useful to consider these questions and answers before planning to deliver this curriculum to students with autism. The guidance is available at: www.bigtalkeducation.co.uk/parents/parents-of-children-with-autism-your-questions-answered/ (accessed 6 February 2020).

Additional sources of further information:

Office for Standards in Education, Children's Services and Skills (Ofsted) (2008) *Looked After Young People: Good Practice in Schools*. Manchester: Ofsted.

Secondary Education, *Supporting Looked After Young People in Your School.* Available at: www.sec-ed.co.uk/best-practice/supporting-looked-after-young people-in-your-school/ (accessed 6 February 2020).

✚ CONCLUSION

This book has provided an overview of the statutory guidance for Relationships Education (DfE, 2019a). It has emphasised the importance of teaching young people to develop caring friendships and respectful relationships. It has highlighted the importance of developing safe online relationships and the need to be a good digital citizen. It has emphasised the importance of young people knowing about different types of identities and relationships, including LGBT relationships and same-sex marriage. In addition, this book has discussed the importance of young people knowing how to look after their physical health and mental well-being.

The guidance addresses subject content that reflects current societal issues. These include sexual violence and exploitation, online abuse, coercion, domestic violence and consent. It is important that schools address these issues so that young people can develop healthy relationships and recognise unhealthy relationships when they occur. It is important that schools address LGBT relationships and same-sex marriage so that the curriculum is inclusive of the needs of all students.

Through the physical health and well-being curriculum which forms part of the statutory guidance, schools also must address a range of controversial topics which may cause conflict with parental values. These topics include drug and alcohol misuse, smoking, healthy eating, physical exercise, social media use, online gambling and debt. Although young people may be exposed to these at home, it is important that young people understand that neglecting to look after one's physical and mental well-being can be unhealthy and lead to illness. Schools should address this sensitively and ensure that young people do not feel stigmatised because of the choices that their family members make.

The Relationships Education guidance offers hope for a brighter future. It promotes the values of respect and care and it highlights the need for healthy lifestyles. It is a powerful curriculum which aims to eradicate prejudice, discrimination and stigma. It reflects the realities of life in modern Britain. It should support young people to lead long, healthy and active lives as full members of the communities in which they live. It supports the development of positive character virtues which will enable young people to form effective relationships and achieve long-term outcomes.

✚ REFERENCES

Department for Education (DfE) (2015)
Sexual Violence and Sexual Harassment between Children in Schools and Colleges. London: DfE.

Department for Education (DfE) (2019a)
Relationships Education, Relationships and Sex Education (RSE) and Health Education: Statutory Guidance for Governing Bodies, Proprietors, Head Teachers, Principals, Senior Leadership Teams, Teachers. London: DfE.

Department for Education (DfE) (2019b)
Character Education: Framework Guidance. London: DfE.

Department for Education (DfE) (2019c)
Keeping Children Safe in Education: Statutory Guidance for Schools and Colleges. London: DfE.

Durlak, J A, Weissberg, R P, Dymnicki, A B, Taylor, R D and Schellinger, K B (2011)
The Impact of Enhancing Students' Social and Emotional Learning: A Meta-Analysis of School-Based Universal Interventions. *Child Development,* 82: 405–32.

Farnan, J M, Snyder, S L, Worster, B K, Chaudhry, H J, Rhyne, J A and Arora, V M (2013)
Online Medical Professionalism: Patient and Public Relationships: Policy Statement from the American College of Physicians and the Federation of State Medical Boards. *Annals of Internal Medicine,* 158(8): 620–62.

Glazzard, J and Mitchell, C (2018)
Social Media and Mental Health in Schools. St Albans: Critical Publishing.

Gutman, L M and Schoon, I (2013)
The Impact of Non-Cognitive Skills on Outcomes for Young People: Literature Review. London: Education Endowment Foundation and Cabinet Office.

Heah, R (2019)
Sex and Relationships Education (SRE) in English Schools: A Children's Rights Persepctive. Unpublished doctoral thesis, University of Liverpool.

Hyndman, B, Benson, A C, Lester, L and Telford, A (2017)
Is There a Relationship between Primary School Children's Enjoyment of Recess Physical Activities and Health-Related Quality of Life? A Cross-Sectional Exploratory Study. *Health Promotion Journal of Australia*, 28: 37–43.

Mavin, S and Grandy, G (2012)
Doing Gender Well and Differently in Management. *Gender in Management*, 27(4): 218–31.

McMahon, E, Corcoran, P and O'Regan, G (2017)
Physical Activity in European Adolescents and Associations with Anxiety, Depression and Well-Being. *European Child & Adolescent Psychiatry*, 26(1): 111–22.

Moffitt, T E, Arseneault, L, Belsky, D, Dickson, N, Hancox, R J, Harrington, H and Caspi, A (2011)
A Gradient of Childhood Self-Control Predicts Health, Wealth, and Public Safety. *Proceedings of the National Academy of Sciences*, 108(7): 2693–98.

NSPCC and PSHE Association (2018)
Making Sense of Relationships. London: NSPCC and PSHE Association.

OECD (2015)
Skills for Social Progress: The Power of Social and Emotional Skills. Paris: OECD Publishing.

Office for Standards in Education, Children's Services and Skills (Ofsted) (2019)
Education Inspection Framework. Manchester: Ofsted.

Pryzbylski, A, Murayama, K, DeHaan, C and Gladwell, V (2013)
Motivational, Emotional and Behavioural Correlates of Fear of Missing Out. *Computers in Human Behaviour*, 29(4): 1841–8.

PSHE Association (2015)
Teaching about Consent in PSHE Education at Key Stages 3 and 4. London: PSHE Association.

Royal College of Obstetricians and Gynaecologists (RCOG) and the Faculty of Sexual and Reproductive Healthcare (FSRH) (2019)
Abortion and Abortion Care Factsheet. London: RCOG and FSRH. [online] Available at: www.pshe-association.org.uk/system/files/fsrh-rcog-abortion-care-factsheet-rse-lessons%20%281%29.pdf (accessed 6 February 2020).

Royal Society for Public Health (RSPH) (2017)

#StatusofMind: Social Media and Young People's Mental Health and Wellbeing. London: RSPH.

Sampasa-Kanyinga, H and Lewis, R F (2015)

Frequent Use of Social Networking Sites is Associated with Poor Psychological Functioning among Children and Adolescents. *Cyberpsychology, Behavior and Social Networking*, 18(7): 380–5.

Scott, H, Gardani, M, Biello, S and Woods, H (2016)

Social Media Use, Fear of Missing Out and Sleep Outcomes in Adolescents. [online] Available at: www.researchgate.net/publication/308903222_Social_media_use_fear_of_missing_out_and_sleep_outcomes_in_adolescence (accessed 6 January 2020).

Taylor, R D, Oberle, E, Durlak, J A and Weissberg, R P (2017)

Promoting Positive Youth Development through School-Based Social and Emotional Learning Interventions: A Meta-Analysis of Follow-Up Effects. *Child Development*, 88(4): 1156–71.

Tiggeman, M and Slater, A (2013)

The Internet and Body Image Concerns in Pre-Teenage Girls. *The Journal of Early Adolescents*, 34(5): 606–20.

Walker, M, Sims, D and Kettlewell, K (2017)

Case Study Report: Leading Character Education in Schools. Slough: National Foundation for Educational Research.

Witt, S (2000)

The Influence of Peers on Children's Socialization to Gender Roles. *Early Child Development and Care*, 162(1): 1–7.

Woodhead, L (2012)

Gender Differences in Religious Practice and Significance. *Travail, Genre et Societes*, 27(1): 33–54.

World Health Organization (WHO) (2018)

Mental Health: Strengthening Our Response. [online] Available at: www.who.int/news-room/fact-sheets/detail/mental-health-strengthening-our-response (accessed 6 February 2020).

+INDEX

131

133

135